HOW YOU CAN FIND HAPPINESS

By SAMUEL M. SHOEMAKER

CONFIDENT FAITH

CALVARY CHURCH, YESTERDAY AND TODAY

CHRIST'S WORDS FROM THE CROSS

THE CHURCH CAN SAVE THE WORLD

CHILDREN OF THE SECOND BIRTH

CHRIST AND THIS CRISIS

THE CONVERSION OF THE CHURCH

GOD'S CONTROL

THE GOSPEL ACCORDING TO YOU

IF I BE LIFTED UP

NATIONAL AWAKENING

RELIGION THAT WORKS

TWICE-BORN MINISTERS

HOW YOU CAN HELP OTHER PEOPLE

HOW YOU CAN FIND HAPPINESS

How You Can Find Happiness

By

SAMUEL M. SHOEMAKER

"I had it in the beginning; and I am more and more coming back to it in the end . . . my original and almost mystical conviction of the miracle of all existence and the essential excitement of all experience."

G. K. CHESTERTON

E. P. DUTTON & CO., Inc.
NEW YORK 1947

FIRST EDITION

For

MY MOTHER

CONTENTS

Introduction

This is not intended to be an abstract book about happiness, but a concrete book which will help people to find it. It is not so much my intention to paint a picture even of what true happiness is, as to construct a practical pathway along which one may travel till he comes to it for himself. One would not add to the already large number of books which put before people big, rather inaccessible visions of what their lives might be. By the thoughts, the attitudes, the beliefs, the practises which are set forth in this book, some of us have come to live in the City of Happiness. All of us move out of it sometimes, but it can become our accustomed domicile. It does not gleam like a tantalizing mirage on the horizon, which only moves further off the nearer you try to come to it: it is as hard and as real as the New York sky-line seen from the Jersey shore, and you can cross into it by just as direct routes. If this book proves to be a little ferry by which even a few people make that transition, it will have been worth all I have put into it.

I always wish my books might be in the nature of a conversation between myself and my readers. Perhaps this is because I spend so much of my time face to face with people in my study, and so am accustomed to

listening. Part of the limitation of a book is that, like a radio talk, it is necessarily a one-sided conversation. But all the time, I am trying to listen to you, as much as if you were in a chair opposite me. As I write, I have in mind a great many types of people—those maritally unhappy, nervously unstrung, fearful, bitter toward life, slaves to others, sick in body or mind, old, weary, bored, uncertain of the future, resentful, as well as the many who, though their lives are averagely satisfactory, are not by any means getting as much out of life as they might be. I wish I knew you personally, knew what made you pick up the book in the first place, knew something of your situation, your aspirations, your life. I cannot hope, of course, to deal with more than the most obvious questions which will arise in the minds of readers, and I know that unfortunately there will be some whom I cannot help at all, with whom I shall be unable to establish that "rapport" which makes two minds meet and not merely skid past each other. But I shall honestly try to put myself in your situation, and to see life through your eyes, and to evade none of the problems which you face. My recipe for happiness, as you will discover, is not found in the optimistic evasions of professional cheerfulness, but that combination of realism plus faith, in the light of which I believe we can find far more happiness than many of us have found. I deeply believe that every person can find more real happiness, if he can find the true adventure which life is meant to be.

There is one serious question which meets me as I write, and you as you read, such a book as this. While we concern ourselves with personal happiness, millions live in the night of hunger, poverty, grinding toil and only the most meager satisfactions. The slim energies left to them after the ravages of war must be spent on the barest necessities—not happiness, but survival, must be their chief consideration. Many of us should be bending far more energy toward relieving the immediate distress, and seeking to build up the economic resourcefulness, of the underprivileged in our own land and throughout the world. In addition to the question whether one has a right to look for personal happiness in a world like this is the further question whether one can truly find it. "How can a life be happy passed in the midst of those who suffer?" asked Sénancour[1]. Do we wrest happiness from life by resolutely shutting out from our emotions the areas of misery and desperation? I know soft and cowardly people who cannot "stand" cancer hospitals, wards of sick children, or the sight of blood or pain: if they think they have found happiness, it is a bogus and unworthy thing—rather they have found a personal ivory tower of retreat.

But there is something more to be said on all this. What we see about us today we charge up roughly to war. And war itself is a result of political break-down, which in turn is a result of moral break-down, which

1 Quoted from *A Naturalist of Souls,* Gamaliel Bradford, p. 35.

in turn arises from deep-seated and unmet anxieties in the hearts of men. War does not just "come," neither is it purely a result of chartable politico-economic causes: men make war, make it because of the misery in life which they feel and for which they have no answer but gigantic hate and aggression, this being the only thing which gives vent and relief to those profound and mostly subconscious emotions which they feel. Hitler got a foot-hold and succeeded because he had an uncanny power to reach and tap and organize the seething resentment, inferiority and fear of his people, turning them first against a scapegoat race within, and then upon other nations outside, his own nation. We have destroyed Hitler, but is anyone naïve enough to think we have done more than cut down a weed of dictatorship, or that we have destroyed the things that made Hitler? They lie deep within the resistful, frightened, bewildered souls of men. There is no telling when or where some other dictator may arise with an even more evil genius, with even more destructive weapons, and exterminate mankind altogether. The precautions being taken against the annihilating use of atomic energy can only touch the surface: there is no precaution against the possible destructiveness of ill-adjusted and unhappy men, with a frightful engine of death in their hands, except to help them find a happier and a better life. When we are dealing with unhappiness, and the problems of personal life, we are not only dealing with the one unit of humankind with which it is possible to deal in a thorough fashion, but we may also be dealing with the great problem of society in the one fundamental way. Philosophers, psychiatrists and scientists will give us strong backing here. Dr. John Macmurray says, ". . . these economic troubles are relatively unimportant. They are not the source of our dilemma, they are merely symptoms. The real trouble lies deeper. We shall never solve our economic troubles till we have solved the dilemma in our spiritual life which produces them."[2] Dr. Howard P. Rome, a psychiatrist of the University of Pennsylvania, recently said that emotional disturbances rooted in fears and tensions are behind the struggle for sovereignty in this world. "It is as if," he says, "suspicious of other men, one is emotionally loath to relinquish any prerogative for fear of total annihilation. This is the stumbling block upon which the United Nations threatens to come a cropper."[3] And Dr. Albert Einstein recently wrote an article in the *New York Times Magazine*, the subject of which was "The Real Problem Is in the Hearts of Men."[4]

If these things be true, we are helping to root war out of the world when we are helping to root unhappiness out of human hearts. It is not all that needs to be done, and we must be always mindful of the contribution which others are making who are dealing

[2] *Freedom in the Modern World,* pp. 17-18.
[3] Reported in the *New York Times,* July 12, 1946.
[4] June 23, 1946.

with society in the large. If one thing in our time is clear, it is that life can never be a circle drawn round the self, nor yet another circle drawn round society: life must be an ellipse round the two centers of self and society. Unless our personal philosophies are related to society as a whole, they become selfish and irrelevant; and unless society is made up of people whose lives are relatively happy and well-integrated, we cannot look for peace in the world. The service which ill-adjusted, unhappy people render to others may be brave, and often is: but it is to some degree suspect. Have we not all seen maladjusted social workers, psychiatrists, teachers, preachers, whose labor for others was a little too obviously the working off of their own conflicts? Our first task is to *be* somewhat, someone. The beginning of the discovery of who we really are, and what we are intended to be and to do, through the release of our tensions and the freeing of our creative powers, is itself the discovery of happiness. Only those who are on their way to happiness can be sufficiently at leisure from themselves to serve others deeply or well.

I believe that the ideas and truths and discoveries reported in this book are real and valid, moreover that they are universal and can be effectual in everyone to a greater or less extent. But I shall seek with all my power to avoid the charlatanry of making it all seem easier than it really is. If it were a light task to find happiness, if there were a button you could press, an idea you could assimilate, a viewpoint you could espouse, if the books which make it seem simple and easy to live victoriously and effectively were true, then there are many tens of thousands of people who would be happy today instead of unhappy. If we are to find our way into the City of Happiness, we may have to alter the course of a lifetime and forswear many of our long-standing customs. It may take nothing less than the transformation of our very selves, if we are to find true happiness; for oftentimes our lives are like a broken arm that has been set the wrong way—it must be broken again in order to be set right. But this process is one that can be known and followed by all of us who want to attain the desired end; and the game is abundantly worth the candle, for there is nothing which everyone craves so much as genuine happiness.

There is one final word that I should like to say. The kind of happiness of which I speak in this book is an active, burning happiness—not a merely passive peace of mind. There can be a contentment which has in it no struggle, and no glory, and may not lie very far from complacency and the "contented cow" outlook.

It was a deep understanding of the true nature of happiness which caused Unamuno, the Spanish philosopher, to close his great book, *The Tragic Sense of Life*, with the magnificent wish, "and may God deny you peace, but give you glory!"

In seeking happiness, one may be falsely led into accepting some things which ought instead to meet rebellion in us; and to endure some things which ought to be cured instead. William James once said that life may not be a fight, "but it feels like a fight." To such a person there can come a happiness of better quality and of greater intensity than to one who merely seeks, and is satisfied with, peace of mind. The presence of this kind of almost flaming happiness was perhaps never more movingly indicated than by Dr. E. Stanley Jones, who said in a recent book, "I don't know of a thing that I want that I haven't got. All I want is more of what I have got."[5] That comes, not only out of rich spiritual service which carries him from one end of the world to the other, on a schedule that would kill most men; but it comes out of a conscious enjoyment of the spiritual warfare itself. Not all have the call or the talents to serve in this same way; but all have both the call and the talents to give themselves to some form of spiritual discovery and service which is so challenging, so vivid and so deeply satisfying, that they with him can begin to say, "All I want is more of what I have got."

S. M. S.

[5] *The Way,* p. 42.

I

Our Present Unhappiness

EVERYBODY wants to be happy. If we are definitely unhappy, we want to be happy. If we are reasonably happy, we want to be intensely happy. It is probable that most of us are both more happy, and less happy, than we think—more happy, if our characteristic picture of ourselves is that of a sinned-against and cheerless person; and less happy, if our customary picture of ourselves is that of a radiant and buoyant person. There are perils and pitfalls in assuming either picture to represent us as we really are.

There are times, also—let us admit it—when we rather enjoy being a bit miserable, even being very miserable indeed. We know those whose stock-in-trade is their aches and pains, their misfortunes, the calamities from which they suffer, who are never so happy as when they are thoroughly miserable and can draw people's attention to themselves because of their misfortunes, this being the only way some people have of mattering to others at all. And do not all of us rather enjoy digging up the forgotten memories of childhood long gone by and never to return, old songs with nostalgia in them that bring a catch in the throat, and sometimes walking in graveyards?

We also know what Robert Louis Stevenson meant when he wrote, "Most men seem to sink at length to the degree of stupor necessary in their different estates. . . . Most men are happy, and most men dishonest. Their mind sinks to the proper level; their honour easily accepts the custom of the trade."[1] There *is* a common complacency and unreadiness to be disturbed, a dumb acceptance of things as they are, which constitutes a kind of spurious happiness. It is a satisfaction with one's state, as against risking any great or costly change, preferring the drab contentment with what is, to the uncertain pursuit of what might be. But this, surely, is not a very intense kind of happiness. Let men once catch sight of real happiness, and they will be discontented with this counterfeit.

But much unhappiness is real. There are literally millions of people who may be said to be unhappy. Something needs to be done about this. There is a passage in Philip Gibbs' *The Hidden City* which runs, "Unhappiness affects the internal secretions. It has an odd effect on the heart sometimes. It lowers physical resistance. It debilitates the nervous system and weakens will power. Sometimes it leads to queer obsessions. . . . It's really quite important to be happy if possible."[2]

It may help us if we understand some of the sources of unhappiness. Some of them are ageless, and belong

[1] *On The Choice of a Profession,* p. 27.
[2] P. 84.

to the experience of life itself—some are peculiar to our present time and situation.

Before seeing the results of a recent nation-wide survey of happiness, published in the *Ladies' Home Journal*,[3] I had put down as the major cause of unhappiness on earth, economic poverty and uncertainty: and I found that the survey backed this conclusion by saying "lack of money tops the list as a source of unhappiness." The survey was made in America, the richest land on earth. Think of the uncounted millions, here and abroad, who will lie down hungry tonight and who never know what it means to be satisfied with enough to eat! What must it be like not to have enough to feed a starving baby, or to provide medicine when a loved one is sick? As one gets near the subsistence-line, fear is added to need. Many a home is unhappy because the parents fear poverty. If America is to make its fullest contribution to a peaceful world, we must do more than back the United Nations Organization, or even create a world-government: we must pour out our gifts to tide starving people over the crisis of this post-war period, and then we must contrive to give them the scientific "know-how" so that they can begin to take care of their own needs. A hunger-ridden, fear-ridden, jealousy-ridden world cannot be a peaceful one.

Ill-health is another age-long and fruitful source of

[3] I am grateful to Mr. Bruce Gould, Editor of the *Ladies' Home Journal,* for letting me see this article before its publication in the September, 1946, issue.

unhappiness. In some cases, one may question which comes first, the unhappiness or the ill-health, so closely are they linked. But good health is almost a passport to a certain kind of joy in living—one's glands manufacture health while they manufacture various interior secretions; while the rack of pain, the ravages of long illness, the almost-pain of great weakness, and the slowing-down of old age, do much to take the shine out of our existence. If we did not believe there is a victorious way of taking these things, we should not be writing this book; but for the record, let it be said that poor health is one of the toughest problems which those who want to live life to the full can meet.

Another abiding well of unhappiness is failure. Growth and advancement in life come by trying tasks which appear to be a little too big for us; we know that it is cowardly, as Phillips Brooks said, to seek "tasks equal to our powers"; rather should we seek "powers equal to our tasks." But sometimes the self-confidence with which we began withers down into a realization that we are not getting away with it. The fear of not succeeding may be enough itself to insinuate a seed of failure in our minds. We may find the task actually beyond us, and have to admit failure. It may come by way of the employer who tells us that our work is not good enough. The shock of having this happen once may be a shattering experience for a delicate spirit; but when it is repeated more than once, when one seems unable to find his or her niche in the world, the wonder sets in, Is there any niche for me at all? The question is not: Have I failed? That is clear—but, *Am I a failure?* Such a thought can devastate people and ruin their lives, if they find no way in which to meet the situation and learn from it.

Further removed from our common consciousness, yet hidden deeper within our real spirits, is the age-old question about life itself. We were born into a world where we did not elect to come. Once our early necessities, mostly material, are taken care of, and the mind awakes, we look about in this mysterious world and universe and begin asking questions. Sometimes we feel that our compact, chattering, busy humanity, living so often in crowded cities, is a kind of protective coalition against a cold and seemingly impersonal universe, just as civilization itself seems like but a clearing in the wilderness (and watch how that wilderness encroaches and overwhelms when you let a place in the country go for a year!). But we get alone—walking at night—in our rooms—especially after something tragic has happened, and the questions will not down. "What are we here for? Where did we come from? Where are we going? What is the meaning of human existence, or has it any meaning?" No one can permanently stave off these questions. They are not theoretical, for upon their answer depends the spirit in which one shall live his whole life—or whether perhaps he shall decide to take his life instead. If we evade them temporarily, they will arise again under some other circumstances. This wistfulness, this wonder, this perplexity—shall it turn into positive and happy faith, or shall it turn into bitter disillusionment and skepticism?

One must let himself face into all the tragic actualities and realize why many come in the end to negative, cynical conclusions. There seems to be enough here to call forth cries of outrage and disgust. Goncourt said, "Life is a nightmare between two nothings." Samuel Butler said, "The utmost that can be said is that we are fairly happy so long as we are not distinctly aware of being miserable."[4] Theodore Dreiser once wrote, "I see life—for most, at least—as a very grim and dangerous contest, relieved at best and but for a very little while by a sense or by an illusion of pleasure, which is the bait and the lure for all to all in this internecine contest."[5] Anatole France said, "In all the world the unhappiest creature is man."[6] And H. L. Mencken says, "To sum up:

1. The cosmos is a gigantic flywheel making 10,000 revolutions a minute.

2. Man is a sick fly taking a ride on it.

3. Religion is the theory that the wheel was designed and set spinning to give him the ride.[7]

Such are the ageless musings of the cynical and unhappy.

[4] *The Way of All Flesh,* p. 220.
[5] *Living Philosophies,* pp. 63-4.
[6] Quoted from *D. L. Moody* by Gamaliel Bradford, p. 95.
[7] H. L. Mencken, *Prejudices III Series,* p. 132.

But there are some sources of unhappiness which are so much exaggerated in our own time that they seem characteristic of it.

We suffer inevitably from disillusionment about the war. Our leaders rallied us with great cries about freedom for all mankind as the war began and continued; and they meant it—these were not only recruiting-slogans, they were the expressions of humanity's greatest aspirations and hopes. Roosevelt and Churchill were eloquent, not only in their own right, but because they spoke out of humanity's deepest desires. But then one saw a deepening slump, an inverse ratio between our progressive victory and our professed ideals; as one came up, the other went down. We find today, not only morals at a low ebb, marriages entered into hastily being no less hastily set aside, and the inevitable post-war turmoil: but we come to the frustrating conclusion that war refers only to the past —it can only put a stop to rampant evil at a given time, it cannot possibly create the new world we want. War only creates a vacuum. We shall put no more in that vacuum than we have character, brains and will to put into it. Our men died only for the *possibility* of a new world, not in order to create it, as the late William Temple never tired of saying.

There is also great disenchantment about human nature itself today. We have come down with a terrible drop from the days, forty years ago, when man thought he was on his way, backed by evolution and his own infinite perfectibility, to a certain Utopia of his own making. Two world wars knocked this into a cocked hat. But we have gone from absurd assurance about human nature to an almost equally absurd disbelief in it. It is true that the war, while it has produced some military leaders of great parts, has not produced statesmen who have been able to relate eternal truths to our times, as Lincoln and Wilson did, words which might keep before us our true goal and destiny. An army WAC writes me, "Most G. I.'s. believe in God, as far as I can see—it's just that many don't seem to have much faith in their fellow-men." When trust is so desperately needed, to come to adverse and negative conclusions about human nature as a whole does not augur well for the future.

We were all conscious that revolution was riding the war, like a crazy man on a wild horse. The totalitarian enslavement which has been checked in Germany and Japan goes on unchecked in Russia, which seems as determined to conquer the world for the Soviets as Hitler was for the Nazis. Our dealing with Russia is a complicated thing; but from what one is forced to believe by reading Kravchenko's *I Chose Freedom* and Brooks Atkinson's, William Bullitt's and John Foster Dulles' articles, it looks as if the professed intention of the Soviets to give the common man economic freedom bogs down in their political enslavement of him. Power and crooked means can blunt the best of ends and aims. Carlyle warned us about the Revolution long ago in words we need to heed today, "Beneath this rose-coloured veil of universal benevolence is a dark, contentious hell-on-earth." When we remember the untold sacrifice of lives in Russia to bring about a greater opportunity for the common man, the unbelievable cruelty and injustice of the continuing system of espionage, the millions in concentration and labor camps, surely little better off than they were in those of Germany, we wonder what lies in store for the world. We do not so much fear for our skins or our property, as we fear what mankind may be called upon to suffer, having been betrayed by the promises of reform and the bright visions which the Soviets dangle before submerged people, only in the end to enslave them like their own. We can hardly help seeing the forces gathering for a gigantic show-down between totalitarianism on the one side, and the nations which believe fundamentally in freedom and the "democratic way" on the other.

We are also forced to admit that all our hopes of education have fallen far below the mark. Thirty-five years ago, I heard a college president say publicly, "Education will save the world!" and my skeptical young mind said, "That is a lie." And it was. On the whole, modern education has robbed the modern mind of faith, only to give it a sterile intellectualism ill-equipped to deal with a world gone wrong emotionally. What power has the average textbook, or classroom lecture, to deal with a spirit like that which ruled until recently in Germany? Indeed, was not the whole Nazi movement a kind of frightful warning to a world which had for too long emphasized the purely intellectual factors, but greatly neglected the emotional ones? What tools does modern education give to a man with which to meet the deep, troubled undercurrents of our time, when it completely begs the question of the deep, troubled undercurrents of his own life? We do fairly well in giving our youth all that the mind can give and take in: but the neglect of the study and understanding of emotion and imagination, and of the subconscious, by modern education, the failure to do what education professes to do, to "see life steadily and see it whole," may eventually prove to have been the great betrayal of our time. Education, like government, can have nothing to do with the propaganda of religion; but both government and education ought to have their eyes open enough to realize that neither of them are safe without the values which religion alone can conserve. Freedom is not safe in human hands unless some other force is at work within humanity to persuade and help the race to use freedom responsibly: and the disinterested and "unmercenary" pursuit of truth, which is the cardinal tenet of the modern educational outlook, is itself a spiritual achievement of a very high order, and apart from the acceptance of values (e.g., of truth, or of the worth of the individual) which are Christian in origin, academic freedom is in danger.

One of the greatest sources of unhappiness in our

time is strained and difficult human relationships. The long separations caused by the war, the discovery of much greater economic independence by women, and the housing shortage, have all contributed to making marriage especially difficult at this time. The loss or lack of standards and values in the average family has taken away any final "court of appeal," so that growing boys and girls do as they please and are uninfluenced by any parental authority beyond the admiration they feel for parents who live up to the things that they ask their children to do. But the inner strain, to which we shall soon come in discussing the unhappiness of our time, takes its toll of daily human relationships, both at home and in business. Because people feel emotionally insecure, inwardly adrift, vaguely dissatisfied, their tempers are sometimes short and those about them feel the edge of their unresolved conflicts. Such people as feel insecure within are most likely to prove dominating and roughshod in their relations with others. They often do this without knowing it, and not until the wife threatens divorce, or the boss tells them that unless there is a change of spirit their services will not be wanted, do they realize how little they have been able to cover up the explosive, emotional condition which lies just beneath the surface.

The most prevalent source of unhappiness in our time is, I believe, the sense that, though we have more to work with than people have ever had before, we have not had the stuff to become the kind of people who could cope adequately with the situation which we are intended to meet. If we were very honest, and put it very bluntly, we would say that we are dissatisfied with ourselves, even that we suffer from self-disgust. We often behave like people with bad consciences, with divided inner lives. Have you noticed in recent years a let-down in our old-time American faculty for cutting through "red tape" and getting things done? It seems to me there is often a stalling, a delay, a "passing the buck," which is not so much due to the inconveniences and shortages of war and post-war times, but at bottom indicates the inability to make a sure and clean-cut decision. Have you ever noticed how many divorced people become divided people—not divided only from the person from whom they have been separated, but divided within themselves—and is not this due to the fact that a divorce is, nine times in ten, a real failure, a breach of promise, which inevitably causes some degree of deterioration in character through a division of emotions, and which leaves the person so much farther from inward integration? Many men and women, also, have gone into commercial pursuits with some degree of idealism; they wanted to be honest, unselfish, decent. Then they found themselves expected to condone or adopt some practise that was a good deal less than honest: and instead of courageously dealing with the matter, ready to take the rap of being fired if that were the price, they have weakly succumbed to the shady practise. It may have kept them their job, but, again, has it lost them their self-respect? There are even people whose self-disgust makes their influence poisonous and subversive. Their inner history is something like this: they met a marriage partner, or a business one, without ever having been cleared of a personal aggressiveness which was born of self-will and inferiority. Other people, "life," meet such aggression with hostility. And this increases the hurt and the aggressiveness, so that all their days these people are motivated (whether they are conscious of it or not) by the desire to *hurt back*, to get even with life; and they sometimes take out their wounded pride in seeking to hurt those who most befriend and seek to help them. These people are both sick and sinful: they need to be surrounded by a very big and understanding love, and then their pride and aggressiveness need to be punctured with a very sharp challenge.

"Self-disgust" is a harsh diagnosis, as sometimes the surgeon's knife is a painful expedient; but if it be the truth, it will be a relief to face it. For "the truth shall make you free." If our accumulated failures, our inability to say that life has taught us any fixed standards or values, our materialism and selfishness, have created in us emptiness and more than emptiness—if they have created in us a real suffering—then we look for a cure, however bitter be its taste. How much physical illness is caused by this inner condemnation of ourselves, it would be hard to estimate. We find that we cannot just leave lightly behind us the shameful things we have done—putting a competitor to the wall, cutting off the connection with a relative or acquaintance whom we do not like, spending on ourselves money dishonestly gained, letting a bitter tongue go unchecked, squandering real talents because we fear to get out of a comfortable groove, being ungrateful to benefactors when we have gotten up in the world—we do not do these things, and then pass on beyond them, leaving them in the limbo of the forgotten. As anyone can go back over the ground and find the foundations undisturbed, after an army has traveled through a country destroying buildings, just so does deliberate and conscious forgetfulness fail to blot out the actual memory of regrettable and reprehensible things. We can sometimes fool our conscious mind, and sometimes we can fool others: but we cannot fool our subconscious minds: there is registered the full memory of what has happened, and the adding-machine of the subconscious has totalled up the score, and is constantly pushing through into the conscious mind, if not the actual score, at least the knowledge that the moral account is distinctly on the red side of the ledger.

Has it occurred to us, for instance, that the real reason why the Russians are behaving so badly about international relations may be due to the fact, not that they are a newcomer among world powers, nor that they do not understand the democratic procedure, nor even that they are playing a long-range game for

Soviet advancement: but that these men are conscious of being in a position which is impossible to defend? Ostensibly they are at work with other nations for the peace of the world, a peace which was only possible after the demon of totalitarianism had been killed in Germany and Japan; but Russia is herself a totalitarianism of the most cruel kind, and the things which are supposed to have been put behind us as we seek a better world are the daily stock-in-trade of the Kremlin. Have you thought that back of the obstructive intransigence of Molotov, and behind him of Stalin, lies the unadmitted consciousness of murder on an almost infinite scale, political imprisonments without number, the torture and fear of millions, all of which lies directly on these men's souls? What wonder if they shy away from those democratic procedures which live on the exposure of the truth, and which, at least at their best, give homage to the God from Whom these men have sought to lead their nation away for more than a whole generation! Is there an impacted moral conviction in these men which makes them behave as they do? And let us not think ourselves free from the same kind of impacted moral conviction. What sham and hypocrisy for us to talk about "de-Nazifying" our zone of Germany, when officers of our own army bring back tons of loot, and millions in stolen jewelry! Shall we not all pay for this brigandage in another generation? It *does something* to people to know that they are the kind of people who do this kind of thing. Outwardly they may become more defiant and aggressive, and even self-righteous than ever: but inwardly they become more self-disgusted and unhappy.

The most dangerous spot for the future of the world is not where they are making atomic bombs: it is where men can find no cover, no relief for the sense of self-disgust which our impotence and failure in face of the gigantic problems and opportunities of our time have given us. We know well that if we had this inner strength, we could stand the trials, and meet the opportunities which are ours. Here is our problem, and here we must seek to find our answer.

II

Ways Out—False and True

WHAT shall we do with the anxiety, the division, the conflict which we find within, and which every so often erupts in fatigue, temper, nerves, incapacity, or sickness? Men have always tried to deal with them, for no one is content to go on suffering from them if relief can anywhere be found. Mind you, much of this suffering goes on below ground, out of sight, in the subconscious: we often steel ourselves so well on the outside that even we are not by any means always conscious of our real unresolved anxiety.

If this sense of life's difficulty or futility becomes too great, if it gets unbearable, the simplest way out may seem to be suicide. Sometimes we get ourselves so snarled up in the tangled skeins of our personal existence that it appears the only thing to do is to cut the thread of life altogether. In ancient times there was a man named Hegesias, who was called by his contemporaries "the orator of death." He belonged to the Cyrenaic school of thought which considered the pursuit of pleasure the only end in life: but he found life so full of cares, its pleasures so transient and so mixed, that he considered death the happiest lot man could seek. He made so many converts to his philosophy that it is said Ptolemy was forced to banish him from Alexandria.[1] We are not likely to take the way of suicide unless all other ways have failed, for there is a fear also of what may lie on the other side of death. But when nothing could seem worse than life now is, when one does not know where to turn for help, when the bottom has dropped out, then some take the way of suicide.

There are many other ways in which we seek relief in less drastic fashion. When the tensions increase many turn to alcohol: it lets the tense nerves down, it brings some temporary cheer into the dark picture, and a "party" now and then seems good fun. The tragedy

[1] *History of European Morals,* Lecky. Vol. I, p. 227.

begins where this cannot be stopped. I know a workman, gifted with his hands, with the soul of an artist yet working as an artisan, who will go along doing his work for months, and then suddenly disappear for days or weeks, lost in the expensive and tragic oblivion of alcohol. Drugs also provide temporarily an escape from the boredom of life or the gnawing of unease in the mind. The dreams and fancies of the unreal world are exciting relief from the awful actualities of the real one—for a time; and, not only those trapped by medical misuse of drugs, but others with their eyes open will sometimes deliberately seek this way of escape. Much indulgence of sex is not a seeking (except secondarily) for affection, but a sheer search for the thrill of sensation to dull or off-set the "basic anxiety," as Karen Horney calls it. Sex in a well-adjusted married life is one thing; but sex sought for its own sake, and not as the fulfilment of an otherwise rounded relationship, is a cheat and a hoax, which promises more than it provides. For some, sport and games, hunting and travelling, eating and other kinds of enjoyment are sought, not only for themselves, but as an escape from this we-know-not-what which seems to drive and pursue us from within. If anybody believes that any of these things offer any solution to this deepest drive in human nature, seeking as it does for the greatest answer, let him listen as I often do to the tragic outpourings of middle-aged sensualists who have given them all a thorough try, and found them deadly wanting!

There are higher ways of seeking a solution. We call them "sublimation." There is our daily work to be done, sometimes drudgery to be sure, but over the long haul there comes much upbuilding of our inner lives from disciplined, daily accomplishment, and the livelihood which is made from it. There is, for most people, a family to be enjoyed and cared for; if we have children, we find satisfaction in seeing them manifest the varied and irrepressible qualities which come out in them, and sometimes to an unfortunate degree we live out our unfulfilled lives through them. Then there is creative art of many kinds, if we have any mind for it; and how many inner conflicts are assuaged by the creation of as much beauty as we can make! Logan Pearsall Smith, a writer of brilliance, spoke of the "solace and consolation of Language," and said, "When I am disconcerted by the unpleasing aspects of existence . . . it is not in Metaphysics nor in Religion I seek for reassurance, but in fine phrases."[2]

Many seek the deep consolations of Nature. Wordsworth almost made a religion of it; and to read him is to remember what the artist Turner said when someone told him he had never seen in nature the lights and colours which Turner put there, "Don't you wish you had?" There is much healing in nature, in the contemplation of its majesty and faithfulness and beauty, in working with it in some corner like a garden, in feeling the renewed health that seems to stream up one's arms from the magic chemistry of the brown

[2] *All Trivia,* Harcourt, Brace and Co.

soil itself. But nature is one of the least satisfactory stopping-places in the world: it is always making you think and wonder what lies within and behind it! Francis Thompson's spiritual search is set forth in his poem "The Hound of Heaven," and is filled with his effort to find in nature what, wonderful as it is, nature does not have to give; and his conclusion is, "Nature, poor stepdame, cannot slake my thirst." How often do people, looking away to distant blue hills and feasting their eyes and resting their souls in them, say, "I will lift up mine eyes unto the hills, from whence cometh my help." But our punctuation is wrong, and so is our philosophy: what the psalmist really says is, "I will lift up mine eyes unto the hills. From whence cometh my help? My help cometh from the Lord, Who hath made heaven and earth."[3] Mountains make a wonderful take-off for the Eternal, but they are no substitute for Him!

I suppose the way that often seems to come closest to "sublimating" the restlessness of the heart is the way of ambition. Nearly all troubled and anxious people are sensitive and inferior-feeling people. Nothing soothes and pleases them like success, followed by appreciation. There are millions of people who would be reasonably happy if from somewhere there were guaranteed to them one good scoop of flattery in every twenty-four hours, as some women keep a standing order for orchids. What is that unaccountable feeling

[3] Psalm 121.

of elation which we carry round after someone has praised an achievement, and why are we so inexplicably cast down when what we thought should have its meed of praise evokes no comment? All of us need appreciation, and should be conscious of the need of it in other people; though we should keep sincere in what we say. But I am speaking now of something neurotic or very near it. How many young men there are who, brought up under the shadow of a strong or critical or inferior-dictatorial father, dream of a gallery of people somewhere in the offing, who will one day applaud them as they come up with great success to their credit, and ask for the praise for which they have thirsted all their days! How many of them work consciously and unconsciously for this more than for anything else! If it comes, even in small measure, it is a very welcome thing. But the trouble with ambition is that, even when its highest rewards are achieved, it still may leave an aching void in the heart. I know a woman who from her girlhood was determined to make her mark and go to the top of her profession; she had stiff competition, but she went to the very top. Said she to me, "When you introduce the President of the United States to your colleagues, you and they know that you have arrived!" But she also said there was an inner void into which she never dared to look, and which was never filled till she found the real answer for her tremendous drives.

There is one other way of "sublimation," looking

very much like part of the true answer, and it is the way of joining up with a group that exists for its own sake. It may be social, like a bridge club: it may be useful, like a service club: it may even exist for religious ends. A group that will provide company for us and satisfy our need for herd-security, a group that will increasingly absorb our emotions and even do our thinking for us, may seem to offer much to its members; but there exists a perilous temptation for its leaders to dominate its members, and for its members to become echoes rather than true and living voices. We sometimes think we have found the way to be happy by immersing ourselves in a political party, a social company, a religious group. But we wake up to find that our unsublimated drives have not truly been sublimated at all, they have only been turned to other ends without being changed in the least. As Nicholas Berdyaev says, "The self-assertion of a group is the form of self-assertion from which there is least hope of escape."[4] Some companies have within them the qualities which permanently help people; others should know when their day of usefulness is done and pass quietly out of the picture. As George Santayana said, ". . . . societies are like human bodies, they all rot in the end, unless you burn them up in time."[5]

A letter lies on my desk from a friend in England

[4] *Slavery and Freedom.*
[5] *Persons and Places,* p. 24.

who writes, "What I should really like to do would be to sit down with you and talk about the curse of fear and guilt that lies like a cloud over people. Psychologists say rightly that there is to be no more condemnation, but they don't see that Christ provided forgiveness so that the fog of fear and guilt could dissolve in the sunlight of God's forgiveness. What they try to do is to get rid of it by saying people are wrong to feel it."

There are three things in that paragraph which can help us.

The first is the reminder of the psychologists that "there is to be no more condemnation." We are our own condemners, and life and events seem to second us in our self-condemnation; therefore we need no more of it from without. Nothing which purports to be an answer for our inward trouble can begin and end by increasing the sense of condemnation, whatever ray of hope may pierce the situation in between: a true answer must begin and end with hope, even though a period of further condemnation may intervene. More condemnation from without, and too long a continuation of that from within, will only add to despair and depletion. We shall be helped here if we realize the difference between *condemnation* and *conviction*, and keep the latter while we do away with the former. True conviction is an honest estimate of where we are, and where we are not, of our failures, our back-slidings from fresh insights and resolves. If it be true conviction, that is, if it comes from the Spirit of God and not from ourselves, then it is antiseptic, clear and (when faced) healing. Conviction is like a clean surgical operation, it gets rid of the source of infection and the wound heals over. Condemnation, however, complains, rebels and suffers from the pain, without going through the healing experience of the operation which removes it. S. Paul gives us one of the soundest pieces of psychological wisdom ever written when he says, "With me it is a very small thing that I should be judged of you, or of any man's judgment: yea, I judge not mine own self. For I know nothing by myself; yet am I not hereby justified: but he that judgeth me is the Lord."[6] That rule, if followed, would do away with "condemnation," of the merely negative, ineffectual sort; but leave us open to "conviction," of the constructive, effective sort.

The second idea here that can help us is to realize the falsity of asking people to stop feeling fear and guilt, by simply sweeping them away. However much the psychologists may believe people are "wrong to feel" these things, we all do feel them. It would be easy for us to say blithely, "Withdraw, you dogs of conviction, and stop barking at my heels. I will not let myself think ill of myself again. I am going to be positive and cheerful." The trouble with this attitude (aside from the emotional impossibility of long maintaining it) is that it throws out the baby with the bath-

[6] I Corinthians 4, verses 3-4.

water—it fails to take into account that part of our self-questioning and self-condemnation which is our given assent to the sense of moral responsibility. If we could throw out our guilt, we should do so at great peril. Every psychologist seeks to arouse at least so much guilt in mentally sick patients, that they begin taking some responsibility for their situation, instead of throwing it all on other people or on "life:" no cure can even begin till some reaction like this is brought about. There is not only poison in our feeling of guilt, there is also promise: the same guilt which means looking backward and inward with moral honesty, means also looking forward and outward with honesty and with hope. If we can do the right thing with the genuine side of our feeling of guilt, and not let it waste itself in idle self-criticism, then we shall find our answer.

The third matter of great importance in that letter is its indication of the answer. "Christ provided forgiveness so that the fog of fear and guilt could dissolve in the sunlight of God's love." Do not now consider forgiveness in any technical or theological sense, and do not let old associations keep you from this new door of hope which may open before you. We know that if once we could get free from the enwrapped accumulations of past failure and unhappiness, if once we could begin again with no counts against us, as if we were starting to live for the first time, we should have a thousand per cent better chance of succeeding. But that is just what God's forgiveness means! There is literally nothing else that reaches way down inside us and touches that burden of shame, fear, unease, distress, and removes it. I wish I could convey to you some sense of the immense and immediate relief of forgiveness, as I have many a time witnessed it in individual people. No mere cheap acceptance of ourselves as we are—no lowering of our ideals—no escape from genuine conviction that we could and should be better —but a glorious sense that we are forgiven and because we are forgiven we begin afresh with a clean slate.

True religion has always recognized the deep need in man for forgiveness. Animal and even human sacrifice in primitive religions (some of them are still operating) arose out of the profoundly felt need for atonement in the human heart. Hear the cry for this in Job,[7] "He is not a man, as I am, that I should answer him, and we should come together in judgment. Neither is there any daysman betwixt us, that he might lay his hand upon us both." We all recognize the demand of God upon us for moral righteousness, and our utter inability to meet it. We cannot confront and bear this thing: another must. The Jews came nearer finding this than any other people, they isolated the need very clearly, they keep a solemn Day of Atonement. If you have ever attended one of their services on that day, as I have, you have felt the most earnest grappling with the desperate need of man for forgiveness: but you

[7] Job 9, verses 32-33.

may also have felt, as I did, that according to this faith man must in the end expiate his own misdemeanors, for his own penitence was his only card. In such a service one feels what an immense distance lies between a Holy God and creaturely, sinful men. What, who, can shorten this distance and span this gap? The Christian belief is that God Himself stepped into the breach and took upon Himself the weight of human wrongdoing. The problem of atonement is the problem of extending to man mercy and a second chance, without setting aside the laws of God: what is called for is some act in which the Divine, while safeguarding His own holiness, offers free forgiveness to man. We believe this was done in the Cross of Christ. Most people will do better to approach all this, not as a theological mystery, but as an attempt to meet a profoundly felt psychological need. We know that our problem with our children is to forgive their wrongdoings *in such a way* that they do not lose the sense of right and wrong when we do it. Ever since Christ died on Calvary, millions have found in Him, not alone the Best Man that ever lived, and not alone the full expression of the love of God; but they have found in Him a Saviour Who saves men by actually forgiving their sins. This is the most thrilling thing that I know! We can come to Him with all our sense of futility, shame, fear, guilt and confusion, and have these lifted off from us as a terrible load is lifted by a derrick. When one is forgiven his sins, as when he is healed of painful sickness, he knows it—knows it throughout the whole of his renewed and grateful being! Not alone the outlook, but the expression of the face, yes, the body chemistry itself, begins to change on the instant of forgiveness. Christ is able to reach down into that whole dark area of confused pride and shame, and bring about humility, gratitude and hope. It is literally nothing less than a miracle—perhaps the greatest of all miracles for us. It has been for many the doorway of hope into the life of genuine happiness for which we are seeking.

Now let me tell you some stories of how forgiveness has become this doorway for several different kinds of people.

A sensitive and intelligent professional man, well along in life, came in to find help. He said he had been all his life a "Galahad-perfectionist." And because he could neither achieve, himself, nor create elsewhere this perfection, he turned to alcohol. For years it defeated him and spoiled his career. Then he got into touch with Alcoholics Anonymous and was greatly helped by them. Yet on occasions he would still go off again. There was one point of the "A. A." program which he had not carried out and which he realized might be causing the trouble. The fifth of their Twelve Steps goes: "We admitted to God, to ourselves, and to another human being the exact nature of our wrongs." There was an old wrong, long gone by, which had lain unforgiven in his memory for several decades. He debated whether he could possibly tell it to me. "I shall never dare to look you in the face again," he said. I told him there were two things in reply to this: as a minister I was commissioned to hear such confessions as his, and to declare to penitent people the absolution of God; as a human being, I was probably in the same boat with himself, and in no position to look down my nose at anybody. He waited a little, and then came out with it. We knelt down and I said the prayer of Absolution, as found on page 76 of the Book of Common Prayer. He got up from his knees a transformed and liberated man. "Of course I can look you in the face," he said: "I never felt like this before in my life." How can anyone hear a story like that, and not realize that the human conscience is terribly delicate and in terribly good working order—here was a wrong more than thirty years past, yet it was as live an issue as if it had happened yesterday, and was never settled until he knew it was forgiven by God!

A woman who had come through several months of psycho-analysis was making excellent progress. One could see the pieces of a divided self slowly coming together under the rarely expert care of a good analyst. I was much impressed with the success of the treatment. She happened to tell me that before the analysis she had gone, on the advice of a social-worker friend of hers, to a clergyman, made a full confession of all the past, and from him received Absolution. She told me, "At that point I let go of all my guilt, and have never felt the burden of it again." What, I wonder, was the possible effect of this thorough confession, and this certainty of forgiveness, upon the success of the analysis? Was not the great work half-done before the analysis began? Yet I hasten to say that her faith, which was strong, was not by itself enough to bring her full understanding of herself and her past experience: she needed the expert scientific help as well. The double cure had begun to take a person so divided that you could hardly tell at one time to which self you were talking, and make of her one whole personality.

Another story was told me by one of my associates. There was in one of the wards of a State Hospital a woman who could not be made to respond to any approach, nothing could rouse her from her apathy and indifference. This minister went to her and talked simply with her about faith, the love of God, and forgiveness. He has a great understanding of mental sickness, and mediates his truth through a very gentle personality and very adroit conversation. At first she would not look at him nor listen to him. But after he had gone away from her bed, she called after him to come back; and then she whispered to him, "The trouble with me is that I murdered my babies." She told him of the way she had done away with unwanted twins. When the full story had poured out, he said to her that, even for this, there was forgiveness from God, if she would receive it. She gave every sign of penitence, and they knelt down and he prayed that she might receive the forgiveness of God. He told me that he assured her of God's forgiveness and that as he left the ward, she waved her hand to him and smiled. Nothing else but this gracious and loving dealing, with the forgiveness of God as its main objective, had been able to carry the least hope to this despairing woman. But this did it. She later left the hospital to return home. How many people, one wonders, sick in body as well as in mind, discouraged and dissatisfied with life, would find just what they seek in a genuine experience of forgiveness?

Part of our problem is to discover an answer which has in it both honesty and hope—honesty about the past and the present, hope about the future. If we are evading the facing of something we despise in ourselves, or if the contemplation of this fact leaves us more despairing than we were before, we cannot have found the answer. The discovery of the divine forgiveness meets this twofold test.

How, then, does this experience of forgiveness come about? It begins when, from somewhere, we catch a vision of faith. It may be the possession of someone else, and seem a very remote possibility for ourselves. It may come through the caring concern of another person, as if life itself were pouring out at least a thin stream of encouragement through the channel of one friendly person. It may begin only with a deep desire for a faith that is greater than what we have. There is immense power in this very looking for faith: for "he that seeketh findeth." One can hardly tell where the seeking leaves off, and the finding begins, for they mesh and merge one into the other.

The next step is an honest appraisal of ourselves. It is of no use to say generally that, of course, we have many faults. The reason why people go to psychiatrists is principally to get themselves sorted out. They often go to ministers for the same thing. It is possible to go to a doctor for a general physical check-up: where shall we go for a spiritual check-up? We need someone who is both sympathetic and honest, who will understand us but not let us down. With such a person we can, in confidence, spread out our lives, our problems, our situation, our faults, our despairs. Such a person will help us to sort out the actual faults and sins in ourselves which have contributed (1) to the creation of our present difficulty, and (2) to taking life's normal difficulties in such a way as to increase and not resolve them. Theoretically, one should be able to give oneself such a moral test: actually it goes better if we will be honest with another person. A young man came in at this point, with a real problem. He knew most of the answers to the problem, in theory; but he needed someone to whom he could "spill" it, someone who would reflect back to him his own deepest convictions and insights rather than give him "direction," and someone who would spread over the situation an aura of hope and expectation. The general opinion is, I suppose, that the more the blame for our predicaments can be put on others, the greater will be our own happiness because we feel free from guilt: but the actual fact is just the reverse. As the *Ladies' Home Journal* survey declared, "It is entirely consistent that the happiest people, who are most likely to seek religion, are also most likely to look to their own traits of character and personality to explain happiness or unhappiness, rather than to trace it to arbitrary fortune. Most of the ingredients of happiness they believe to be matters within their own control. The happy person thinks the individual, not fate, is responsible for his own happiness or lack of it." Hence the necessity for this fearlessly honest appraisal of ourselves. Take the Sermon on the Mount, for example, in St. Matthew, chapters 5, 6 and 7, and as you see there an ideal or principle, write down where you fail in living up to it. Tell this in candour to another person you can trust, and see if he can help you find other failings which you had not noticed. Rate yourself honestly—that is the first step.

Then tell God simply that you are sorry. I have been with many a person when they prayed out that first prayer for forgiveness—often the first one they ever said out loud, or with another person. The more general the confession, the less sure the sense of forgiveness and consequent change in life: the more specific and detailed the confession, the more sure the sense of forgiveness and the certainty that God had somehow come in through this doorway of penitence and confession. This ought to be as natural as it is for a child having done wrong to come and say so to its parents. If they are the right sort, they will be very accessible, very sorry with him for what has happened, very much identified with him and not aloof or critical as though they did not sin themselves, and very sure that he realizes it is God he must reckon with, more than parental disapproval or punishment. This attitude of adherence to moral principle, yet of sympathy and hope in the light of forgiveness, is a reflection of God's attitude to us, when we come to Him in penitence. He welcomes us, He is saddened by our wrongdoing, He is ready to receive our honest admission, and He is ready to forgive and to restore. If you don't believe that, carry out this process step by step, and see what the result is!

And then we must remember that we need forgiveness again and again. The first big step through the doorway of confession leads into a new life, and there is no doubt about it: the resultant freedom and optimism and sense of growing faith testify to it. But this does not mean we have stepped across a magic line into perfection. If it takes a long time to root out even an evil habit (though sometimes a thing like drink, or other moral aberration goes at once, and for good), how much longer an attitude in the subconscious! Once I used to wonder why religious people went on Sunday after Sunday confessing the same old sins in the same old way: but now I see it is the only thing that fits the situation. We are inclined, either to slip back into old faults (never, however, without the memory that we have been freed from them for a time); or to experience pride pushing up through moral success, and making moral failure out of it—then the pride must be broken all over again and a new forgiveness asked for. The happiest people that I know are the people who never pretend to be more than they are, who make great spiritual claims for their faith but never for themselves, who keep strict and short accounts with God by admitting to Him every time they have gone off the path. This does not take a long time, it becomes an habitual attitude. But it prevents the accumulation of small or great wrongs which finally become so great we cannot carry them.

One could wish many things for this distracted world of ours. But I think the thing I most crave for it is a great bath in the love and forgiveness of God. I am sure that nothing else goes to the center of the human problem and gives man the answer to it. This way lies happiness!

III

The Happiness Which We Seek

WHAT is the nature of happiness?

Let us take a quick trip back into history. Aristotle believed in something he called *eudaimonia*, which means happiness, and he thought pleasure was secondary to this and included in it. The Stoics believed character, duty, discipline and virtue represented the supreme "good" of life. The Epicureans believed that happiness was the whole aim of human endeavour. This did not necessarily mean sensuality, though it frequently degenerated into it. Epicureanism could be refined, and rest not on material goods nor pleasure, but on moderation in pleasure, and in the right use of the mind, reflecting often upon beautiful acts. But "enlightened self-interest" which is a favorite theme of Epicureanism does easily become a disregard of the rights of others. Immanuel Kant believed that morality and happiness were inseparably connected: he also believed that God and a future life were inseparable as beliefs from the moral law which reason imposes upon us; and thought we must obey the "categorical imperative" of the moral law not in order to be happy, but just because it is the moral law. One's actions, he taught, must be such that everyone could follow your principle of action. These basic themes as to what constitute happiness, and many variations of them, occur again and again in history. Spinoza said that the three things men want are riches, honour and lust. Never, perhaps, has the Epicurean view been more wittily stated than by H. L. Mencken, when he wrote:

"To be happy (reducing the thing to its elementals) I must be:

"a. Well-fed, unhounded by sordid cares, at ease in Zion.

"b. Full of a comfortable feeling of superiority to the masses of my fellow-men.

"c. Delicately and unceasingly amused according to my taste."

One cannot escape the feeling, somehow, that these men were analyzing a living thing as if it were a corpse, and talking at a distance of something they had not greatly experienced in their own lives.

What, then, is happiness? Let me tell you some things which I think it is.

Happiness is *absorption.* I have a friend who was for many long years an invalid, until an experiment by a great brain-specialist with a new drug made her a perfectly well woman. After she was white-haired, and the early and middle years of her life were behind her, she found that the hidden talent and desire of her life was to paint. She began taking lessons and made rapid strides, traversing quickly what might have been spread over many years. She spends long, long hours of every day before her easel, she grudges almost every hour that must be spent elsewhere in sleeping or eating. She has completely lost herself, and found herself, in the absorbing, fascinating, all-engrossing work of painting. I have often remembered the remark of one of my professors, Dr. Dickinson Miller, that the best picture he knew of happiness was children under a Christmas tree. The lights, the tree in the unusual place, the presents, draw out every focussed power the child possesses; you can hardly distract him or get his attention for anything else. He is lost, and found, in his perfect absorption in the Christmas tree.

Happiness is the sense that one *matters*. We are always fighting for the consciousness of importance. Unless we feel it, about our work, and about our lives, we are strangers to happiness. We find, however, that this road to importance is one that soon divides, and goes in two directions. One way we realize that the final estimate of how much we matter must be left, not only to others but to those few others who are in position to speak both understandingly and justly; and that no human being can quite make a fair estimate, so that we must leave the final reckoning to God. The other way, we simply create our importance in our own minds, and make our thirst for it the grounds for assuming it. The safest course, I think, is to seek to *matter to other people*, in the way of loving and serving them. The world is so full of little tiny people, living for little tiny considerations—how can their lives be made to count, so that they feel they matter? Not by being great and rich and influential, as the world counts these things; but surely the way of unselfish service is open to them, and sometimes achieves for them far greater importance than they could possibly achieve in any other way. We know how necessary it is to take seriously what children intend seriously: the same applies to the lives of all people, big or little.

Happiness is an *abiding enthusiasm*. Making the tour of Westminster Abbey many years ago, I heard another tourist say to the verger who was showing us round, "This place thrills me!" To which the benign old guide replied, "Yes, madam, but you can't thrill for thirty years!" Now that is just where he was wrong. Because later on I met another verger, M. Houvet, of Chartres Cathedral, standing rapt in wonder as he beheld the slanting rays of the setting sun through the miraculous windows of the great cathedral, gazing as if he had never seen this splendour before. Then I knew that you could "thrill for thirty years," if you have a great enough thing to be thrilled about, and if you are a person who does not let your power to thrill be dulled. No passing thing can provide this permanently. We must have our wagon hitched to a star that time cannot move, we must have our anchor let down in deep water, we must occupy ourselves with the things that are eternal, if we are to keep that happiness which is an abiding enthusiasm.

Happiness is *single-mindedness*. Nobody, of course, can have only one thing in his mind at a time, not if he lives in New York at least! But he can be free of those inner divisions which cut him into two if not more people, and make his inner life give forth sounds like an orchestra tuning up. He can achieve an inner unity, and he can seek after a great, inclusive goal that will absorb all his powers. William MacDougall says, "Happiness arises from the harmonious operation of all the sentiments of a well-organized and unified personality, one in which the principal sentiments support one another in a succession of actions, all of which tend towards the same, or closely allied and harmonious ends."[1]

Happiness is *whole-heartedness*. Dr. Karen Horney gives, as the conditions for the building up of self-confidence, the following: "aliveness and availability of one's emotional energies, the development of authentic goals of one's own, and the faculty of being an active instrument in one's own life."[2] The really happy people, as I observe them, are the head-long people. The half-pagan is miserable because he is also half something else. The half-Christian is miserable because he is half something else. We are reduced to going the whole way with the life of pleasure, or with the life of the Spirit—and the whole way of the life of pleasure

[1] *Social Psychology*, p. 156.
[2] *Our Inner Conflicts*, p. 100.

leads to some kind of misery in the end—ask the man who's tried it! Let me give you one or two quotations from Dr. William E. Hocking: "Psychologically speaking, happiness may now be described as the continuous *undivided* consent of my whole-idea to the experience or activity at hand; and the empirical mark of happiness is concentration, or enthusiasm of action. To the happy man, things and deeds appear worthwhile: his actions meet the mark, and rebound to enhance his energy for the next stroke; whereas those of the unhappy man strike, if at all, like spent bullets, or shatter, and contribute nothing to his self-continuance. Whatever restores wholeness in action restores happiness. . . . Happiness does certainly not depend immediately on external things at all, but upon our inward mode of dealing with them. . . . The type of attention requisite for happiness seems to depend on a belief during the course of any effort that the object thereof is *worth* my whole devotion. . . . To 'get into the game,' accepting its rules and its risks, has been given as the best available rule for human happiness . . . we know that defeat, if it comes, as it always may, will not destroy our integrity of spirit, and therewith our happiness."[3] I think back to my own hours of most intense happiness—writing as I am this minute on my typewriter, listening to some story of human bewilderment and need and with the teller beginning to find the answer, visiting my people in their homes, absorbed in

[3] *The Meaning of God in Human Experience,* pp. 492-4.

a great book worth reading, or digging in my garden—and in every case "whole-heartedness" is the best description one can give of what is taking place.

This brings me to one of the most important things that must be said about happiness. And that is that *happiness is a by-product.* This is what underlies Walter Lippmann's remark that "the pursuit of happiness was always a most unhappy quest."[4] The point is, if you seek happiness directly and for its own sake, the thing eludes you. Did you ever try to look straight at a very bright star? You probably found it difficult to see: but if you looked a little to one side of it, you saw it much more clearly. You must look to one side of happiness, if you are to possess it. People who feel they have a "right" to be happy seldom are happy. We are free citizens of a free country, and the "pursuit of happiness" is listed in our Declaration of Independence as one of our inalienable human rights: but this must be taken in a political sense, that man shall have the freedom to determine the outline of his own life—it does not mean that because he is free to seek for happiness, he will necessarily find it. We have no "right" to demand of others such acquiescence or conformity with our wishes as we may think will bring happiness to us—for, while it is out of order to think about our own "right" to be happy, it is very much in order to remember the "right" of others to be happy. We shall probably miss happiness if we seek it as our due. Hap-

[4] *A Preface to Morals,* p. 4.

piness is more likely to be found in the relinquishment of our rights than in the exercise of them. We must busy ourselves safeguarding the "rights" of others, and equally we must remember that, because happiness is a by-product, we cannot seek it directly for ourselves. The woman who has found her destiny in painting, the verger at Chartres, a woman who just came in with flowers for someone who is sick—none of these were seeking happiness: they found it as the by-product of doing something else that was interesting and useful.

And happiness is *faith*. Life is a series of fragmentary experiences, coming in rapid succession one after the other. They lack cohesion and possible plan unless there runs through them some thread that binds them together: if no such thread exists, we simply cannot be happy. The integrity of sound human character, meeting each successive event with an unchanged face and an unswerving set of values, constitutes one important thread: but even if one may succeed in weaving some pattern of the events of his own existence, neither this nor the sum of all personal patterns can give to the *whole* of existence the unity and purpose upon which happiness must in the end rest. I do not see how anybody can look with a calm spirit upon the immeasurably great suffering of this very hour, unless he believes that there is in this universe a Power with ultimate good for its intention, and unless he can find place for suffering and tragedy within, and the way toward, the ultimate good. I quote Dr. Hocking again, for he says it better than anyone else I know: "Let me but know or believe in some power that is controlling or shall control physical event and history; then the event begins to have a meaning: and I can find my happiness in the assured victory of that power. . . . History has entered into the absolute goal of things as a member; and all history thereby becomes contributing and important. . . . It must be possible, then, for our wills . . . to contain the will of the universe. We must be able to reach a kind of maturity in respect to God himself, in which we are ready to assume the burden not only of omniscience—as we continually do—but also of omnipotence, with regard to some fragment, however minute, of the historical work of the universe. In such a moment the act which we should utter would be known as a completely real act; and since we cannot separate our own reality from the reality either of our objects, or of our deeds—we too become for the first time completely real."[5] We shall have more to say later on about how people can find this faith which constitutes so large a part of happiness.

Thus far we have been speaking of the general nature of happiness. Of course, this does not exist in a vacuum of isolation. We must now go on to speak of some of the places where happiness is found and expresses itself.

[5] *The Meaning of God in Human Experience,* William E. Hocking, pp. 496, 502-3.

For instance, in the home. What is happiness in married life, in the family? We meet a person, and suddenly or gradually realize that this is "the" person. Friendship ripens into love, and we are married. For some the twining of two wills into one is rather a natural experience: they are good-natured, calm people to start with, much has been talked out before, and genuine unselfish love does the rest. But for many this is a great hurdle—like the couple who came into church, went up to the altar and the minister made them one: then they got into their car, and the question soon arose, *Which* one? Soon or late the merely emotional factors, important as they always are in marriage and the home, are replaced by the character factors. In the long run, we want something more than romance: we want dependability, honesty, patience, carefulness in responsibilities, graciousness toward people, deep integrity. Marriage is meant to develop from burning romance into steady understanding. But this presupposes something of what we mean by character. None of us is perfect, and we ought to realize that marriage is meant to train and develop us in mature living and to get at our faults, expose them and cure them. This calls for maturity, it is threatened by irritable self-centeredness, it is undermined by irresponsibility and selfishness. How many people marry on the basis that this is the person who *can make me happy?* Such a marriage is on dangerous ground from the start. Dr. Smiley Blanton says that the problem in marriage is not to *find* the right person, but to *be* the right person. We shall have more to say that bears on this subject when we come to consider human relations in general.

And how about the job? Suppose it is boring to us now! There must be millions to whom work is irksome, and it is a tragic thing that so many men will accept a government dole when they could work if they would. One of the worst things that has happened to America is the growing dislike of work, as if it were menial as if amusement, leisure and pleasure were the real aims of life. We all ought to love to work, love to do *our work*. If we are fairly young, let us make as thorough a canvass as possible of our capacities and interests and of the work in which these might best find fulfilment. Psychological tests may help us but should be hardly determinative by themselves. If we are to enjoy our work, we must believe it worth doing: therefore we should consider not only where our talents may lead, but where the need of the world may call. This means we should pray much about it, pray with minds and hearts open to God, to show us where He wants us to be, where in His great scheme we fit. If we are in a place we feel to be the wrong one, even if we are middle-aged and have a family responsibility, we ought to consider carefully doing something else; there is no virtue in drudging along all our days in something which we dislike. On the other hand, maybe what is needed is not another job, but a fresh way of looking at the one we have. Is it not the general view of daily occupations that the main thing is the work to be done, and that others who work with us are mere instruments to get it done? The people I find getting the most satisfaction out of their jobs, and often doing the best quality of work in them, are people who put those with whom they come into contact first, and the job second. I do not mean they take company time to talk and gossip, or are inattentive to the calls of the work: I mean that they cease to think of themselves or their colleagues as adjuncts to the job, and begin thinking thoughtfully, creatively about them as people. There is always friction arising in offices and plants: to make friends with someone who has a chip on his shoulder, gain his confidence, find out what is troubling him emotionally, and help get his problems talked over—this is both a fascinating experience in itself, and benefits everybody concerned. The worker enjoys his work more because his life is happier: the employer is happy because more work, obviously, is done by contented people than by discontented. There is much satisfaction in doing well a piece of work one has undertaken, however small or unimportant it may seem. There is more satisfaction in improving one's own methods, getting more and better work done for less expenditure of energy. There is much more satisfaction in reducing the amount of friction and social tension in a human situation, and so improving the health and happiness, the quality and quantity of output, of one's fellow-workers. So—let us try to find the right job—the job God wants us to do. If we have missed it, let us see whether we should make a change and find it. Let us ask for imagination to see the daily "grind" in such a fresh way that it takes on newness and even romance. And let us begin being much more conscious of the people about us, seeking in small ways to help them, spreading throughout the working force a spirit of "give" instead of "get." It is surprisingly contagious!

Money also contributes to people's happiness. The *Journal* survey said some interesting things about this. It said, for instance, that "if your income is equal to the average—about $2,100 a year—your chances of being happy are the same as those of a person receiving many times as much." It also said that happy people place money only in the fifth place as a source of happiness. There are two points that I should like to make about money. The first is that many people are not making as much as they could, because of personality and character-traits that are unfortunate and keep them in the lower brackets. We all know what an important factor "personality" is in making a good income. But "personality" is partly a born and given quality, and partly an achievement. Many over-quiet and somewhat inferior people, when they are loosed from their prison of self-consciousness, are personable and attractive people. Many who fail to "sell" themselves because of their aggressiveness, when they are helped to see the hurt, or the resentment, or the inferiority, or the pride, which underlies the aggressiveness, cease to be aggressive—and do a much better job. There are uncountable buried talents in most people, capacities which an ambitious subconscious self sometimes proclaims with frustrated rage, and which can express themselves when these people are set free by ways which are perfectly well known and open to them. It is one of the chief aims of this book to suggest what they are; for this release of the real selves of people is a principal part of happiness itself. Free, released people make a better impression, are given larger responsibilities, and generally bring home more bacon, than other people do. We cannot make small capacities into great ones: but we can be sure we have developed our capacities to their full limit.

The second point I want to make about money is that, like most things, our attitude toward it is more important than the thing itself. We have all known people with a good deal of money, who because of worry, meanness, extravagance or poor stewardship were always talking poor, and who really were poor because that was the way they felt. We have also known some people who had little money, but who had also a kind of wealth in the mind, and an attitude toward money which gave no one the impression that they felt poor or were poor. One cannot feel this way if he is avaricious, or jealous of others who make more than himself, and unless he can have it as a fixed conviction that there are other values in life than money.

As I write, I have come from a visit to a barber who has been in his present job for fifty-two years: it is in the shop of a fine old club, where he has always come into contact with nice people. He said to me, "Look what a nice room I have worked in all these years, and think of all the nice men I have known! I've had my ups-and-downs, and I haven't made as much as some people. But I have raised a family, and have my house, and I keep a riding horse. There's a lot else in life besides money!" He kept telling me what a happy life he had had. The happiness wasn't in the income, it wasn't even in the job: it was in the barber! Let the would-be millionaires and the rolling stones reflect a little upon the values in life that he has discovered!

We begin to see, then, that happiness is not always having things our own way, nor always being free from anxiety and trouble, nor living in circumstances that are ideal. Such a sugar-sweet existence would probably be cloying and eventually distasteful, if life were so arranged that it were possible: but fortunately it is not. Happiness consists much less in having fortunate things happen to us and round about us, than in finding the right way to take these things. Which will give us a sense of really having lived—to escape as much difficulty and trouble as possible, or to know that we have shared in the common lot of man, but been given an uncommon amount of what-it-takes with which to meet that lot? To have some understanding of the given and unchangeable nature of our existence in this world, to accept the facts of our personal existence which cannot be altered, to know both the genius and the limitations of our capacities, to realize that we did not make life nor this world and cannot expect to understand them as well as their Maker, nor to do as well in meeting them without His help as with it, to seek therefore to discover what He wants and wills us to do in given situations, expecting from Him power as well as inspiration, to know that, as concerning us, our nation, our world and our time, "the event is in the hand of God," and to believe that this world does not see the end of our personal existence, as it does not see the triumph of justice nor the ultimate victory of those truths and values which make life precious and glorious, but that we are set for an eternal life—this, it seems to me, is of the essence of human happiness.

IV

The Greatest Source of Happiness

THE man who made the *Ladies' Home Journal* survey on happiness told me that while ordinarily these surveys tended to confirm the obvious, the results of this survey surprised him considerably. The great surprise was the information contained in these words:

"Happy people are religious people! The very happiest people found in the entire survey—those who meet every important test of happiness—go to church more often and are far more likely to look to religion for comfort and help, than the rest of the population. This is so marked that the chances of being happy and not religious are pretty slim; 86 per cent—nearly nine in ten—of the happiest people say that they get much consolation and help from their religion. . . . Wealth and advanced education, which are not accessible to most Americans, are not widely characteristic of happy people; but religion is, and it is available to anyone willing to accept it. And religion means more than going to church; it is also a matter of accepting the support that religion has to offer."

Now let us see what real religion is, and how it is turned from aspiration into possession for ordinary people today.

Real religion, at its best, is not so much an attitude, nor a set of values, nor a philosophy, nor even a way of life: religion is a current of power. The Great Teacher said that the summary of the law was to love God and to love others. Love is not a static, but a dynamic thing. Did love ever look out of the eyes of a statue, or remain inactive as an attitude? No—love is like a current of electricity. And religion is being in the mid-stream of that current. Mainly it runs through three centers: God, others and ourselves. You can't be in real relation to God unless you are in real relation to others; and you can't be in real relation to others unless you are in real relation to God. Religion is not shaped like a sling-shot, with ourselves as the handle, and then two prongs reaching out, one to God and the other to other people: religion is more like a triangle with a current of electricity running through the three angles, God, ourselves and others. I have found this simple picture helps people: God is like a dynamo—He is unseen, but He is the great Source of power. God, to be accessible to us, must have an outlet, where we can get in contact with Him. Jesus Christ and His churches are the accessible outlets of God in the world, just as available as the outlet in your floorboard if you would attach your lamp to the invisible dynamo. The plug which fits into the outlet is our part in setting in motion this current of power: God does not force Himself upon us, though none of us can escape from His laws—we will to get in touch with Him, and we do it by the surrender of ourselves to all of Him we understand. That is how people "plug in" and get going. Our lives are meant to be the lamps. The outlet is the dynamo brought closer to the lamp, and the plug is the lamp brought closer to the dynamo. Now all this may be just a set-up, just a good piece of wiring *unless the power is on.* The current is always potentially on, but it is not actually on until we are praying to and working with God. Prayer, in some mysterious way (no more mysterious than electricity), turns on the switch of power, and we know we are in touch because of the light that illumines, the power that energizes, and the warmth that kindles our lives.

Take another figure. An anxious, overconscientious woman sat fidgeting and disturbed. She wanted the power of God in her life so much that she was so strained that she couldn't find Him. I said, "Let's think of your life as a ship. You are very busy trying to get up a big head of steam, in order to carry a big cargo of work to its destination. This may be the fulfilment of a picture you have of yourself as a highly capable, conscientious professional woman. Now the first and chief thing about a ship, before there is any steam or cargo or motion, is that it rests on a great bed of buoyancy called the ocean. Before it can go anywhere, a ship must let itself down completely into the water. Before you can go anywhere, you must let yourself down completely into the great bed of buoyancy which is the love of God." You may remember that magnificent vision of George Fox, the founder of the Friends: in the midst of civil war in England he wrote, "I saw that there was an ocean of darkness and death in the world, but I saw that there was an infinite ocean of light and life and love that flowed over the ocean of darkness, and in that I saw the infinite love of God." It is not our task to create the current of power, nor the ocean: but only to come close enough to be carried along by the one, and buoyed up by the other. Self-effort religion, "boot-strap" religion, has about run itself out: the day has come when we must begin with the greatness and goodness of God, remembering that His concern for us is greater than our concern for ourselves. This is the great encircling, under-girding, over-all fact.

But we shall find that some things we do can turn off the current, and prevent our letting ourselves down into the love of God in faith. We may have found that long-protracted giving in to faults and foibles, to self-indulgences and personal whims, has so dulled our spiritual sensibilities that they need a deal of toning up before we can do anything. Christianity, it has been said, has a moral back-bone. When we see and admit how that back-bone has, for us, gone to gristle, or even to jelly, we shall begin to awaken to spiritual things. A headmaster said to me recently, "We have got to get some moral values back into these schools. We have got to let these boys know that stealing is stealing, and adultery is adultery." S. T. Coleridge said, "Do you in good earnest aim at dignity of character? . . . I conjure you . . . turn away from those who live in the twilight between vice and virtue."[1] If we could get people out of that moral no-man's land and get them to call wrongdoing by its real name, we should not be contributing to the tension of people today, but lessening it. It is a fact that, as someone said, "we take hold of God by the handle of our sins." This is what is called the "nonic" approach; many things are well-described by what they are not: and God is best

1 "Aids to Reflection: Sensibility."

found by discovering from what parts of life He has been banished. After a long and varied search a friend of mine has found spiritual security and serenity: an honest letter says, "God knows I've sinned most of my life and I still get angry and irritable and intolerant: but at least I know it. There has never been any grey for me, things have always been black or white; and they aren't grey for my children. They see straight, and if they do wrong, at least they recognize it for what it is, they don't white-wash their faults and pretend it's all right." I think there is a connection between this moral honesty and realism, and coming out finally into the light of real, living faith.

Now it is not enough merely to be honest about past or present wrongs. The first thing is to see and know what constitutes sin for us: whatever walls us away from God or from others surely falls into this category. The next thing is to face up to the wrongs that have been or are in our own lives. This is an exceedingly difficult thing to do, one in which we may need the expert help of a spiritual or psychological counselor: for, as we shall see later, most of us are quite ignorant of ourselves, and one portion of us spends a good deal of time rationalizing ourselves into thinking that whatever we want to do is all right. Then we need to confess these things to God, in all candour. There is a real difference between what happens to a person spiritually who generally admits that he or she is "a sinner," and one who specifically asks God's forgiveness for this, and this, and this, naming the thing by its actual name. And there is yet another step: where our wrong has hurt another, we must go to him in honest admission and seek to make it right. No matter if most of the wrong be on his side—let us admit the wrong on ours, and it may start a contagion of honesty. Have you ever known the cleansing, the lightening of the emotional load, that comes when one is simply and humbly honest with another where one has been wrong? And do you know how an apology left unspoken, a restitution left unmade, an old debt left unpaid, becomes the kind of "unfinished business" which works its way back and may spoil the spiritual beginning that has been made? We want to find happiness—don't we?—all the happiness there is. Well, that old impacted conviction will be like a toothache when you are ready to go to a party! It so happens that wrongdoing and unbelief are sworn allies: and one abets the other. A delightful young pagan said to me, "I don't believe in God." I said, "Well, that might be due to two things: (1) you may despair of yourself to date, consider yourself actually incorrigible, and you rationalize this into a theory that there is no hope, therefore no God; and (2) you know that if there is a God, He wants you to live a mighty different life from the selfish one you are living at present; and so it is less disturbing not to believe in God than to believe in Him—just now." There came a frown—then a smile—and then the words, honest as sometimes the pagans are so delightfully honest, "I think you may have something there!"

But the finding of God—how does that come? How do we "plug in" at the outlet and get the light?

Let me first say something about the One I described as the outlet. I mean Jesus Christ. I venture to say that most of us look upon Him as the best the world ever saw, the teller of perfect parables of truth, the greatest influence for good of the centuries. One can start here: you remember Demetrius in *The Robe*[2] saying to Theodosia, "I don't know what I believe about this Jesus. I never saw anyone like him: that is as far as I can go." He is very patient with such attempts on our part to estimate and assess Him: in fact He will just stand there waiting till the balance shifts, and we begin to realize that He is estimating and assessing us—for He is either, as Kierkegaard said, the cause of our being offended in Him, or else He is the object of our faith—in either case the initiative and overture come from Him. For those who accept Him as the Object of faith, their belief is that the truths and secrets and drama of the universe itself were writ small for man to read in the whole episode of Jesus: its purpose, its mystery, its tragedy, its glory, all completely rescripted, summarized, clarified, transfigured, in that one Life. For me He is not only the guide and guarantee, but the very picture and essence of truth and reality and God. As His life is greater than all its con-

2 P. 202.

sequences, so it is greater than all the truths He revealed and uttered. Our souls fly like free birds among the ample branches of the great tree of His truths: they come only to rest in Him. There is no question of "what I shall do" with such an One, but only of "what He will do" with me. He is the very incarnation, not only of God, but also of the only true happiness this world ever saw. Did they call Him a "Man of Sorrows"? Yes, and He was that, through His compassion for all the sons of men, and the burdens they bear and the blindness from which they (often needlessly) suffer. But what must be His deep gladness Who always brings gladness to all who come to Him, and Who did always the things which pleased His Father?[3]

As for what constitutes our own "plugging in," we begin just by beholding Him. S. Paul says, "We all, with open face beholding as in a glass the glory of the Lord, are changed into the same image. . . ."[4] A child takes colour from those about him: influence by contact is the surest, most inevitable thing in the world. The best thing we can do is to *stay around* Jesus—read His words and His life, go where His people gather, and keep looking at Him. Someone asked an old French peasant woman what she did in church? She said "Oh, I just look up at Him, and He looks down at me." Try that awhile! Alfred Whitehead says, "Moral education is impossible without the

[3] St. John 8:29.
[4] II Corinthians 3:18.

habitual vision of greatness." Then let us take the supreme vision of unique greatness, and keep looking at Him. Slowly, steadily, inexorably not our gaze only, but our lives, will go over to Him, and be ours no longer. One day when we have done all our questioning and rationalizing, all our holding back and kicking against the fact that life is as life is, and Christ is what Christ is, and quit all the childish and petulant and self-defeating things that we do to keep from coming to grips with the only thing that can ever save us from ourselves, or bring us any measure of happiness in this world, we shall simply let go, and ask Him to take us over, and forgive us, and transform us, and re-make us as He would like to have us. The relinquishment of our wills to Him is the jolt which starts this process on our side; later we shall find He has been drawing us all the while, and but for His power to draw us, we should never have had the strength to make the liberating decision.

There are sometimes two steps involved in what is called a "Christian decision." There is, first, what might be described as a surrender to Whatever-is-the-truth. This is a moral step, implying dissatisfaction with the past, and the determination to live a different and a better life in future, with the aid of whatever beneficent powers above the human there may be. God is very great: let none forget the greatness or the mystery of Him. There are some who do not feel at liberty to call themselves Christians, because they are as yet too undecided, too modest, to go so far. Many of these people are among the most earnest spiritual seekers of our time: we must welcome their search and acknowledge their honesty and reach out to them in appreciation. They have decided it will not do to leave their life gears in reverse, for this leads backward into self-centeredness. Perhaps they cannot yet push their gears up into the high of full Christian conviction. But they are wise enough to put them in neutral. Take hold of the gear-shift in your car, and wiggle it to see how light and free it rides there—that is the way the soul must be as it seeks to move up out of the reverse of the ego into the high of full Christian faith! Many a man has had to build an altar in his heart "to the Unknown God," and rest content with this tentative worship till the greater truth breaks upon him.

But then there is the second step, of self-surrender to Jesus Christ Himself. We have looked long for the inner meaning of the Truth to which we have given ourselves, and we find that Truth defined and incarnated in Jesus. One may come to this conclusion upon historical or philosophical grounds, or upon the grounds of personal experience, believing that He proves His mighty claims by what He actually does for us. It is often true that, as we surrender to all we understand of Truth, we are led on to more Truth; and the Unknown God becomes the Known God. And for many millions through the centuries, the Known God is Jesus Himself.

This experience is really what Christ was talking about when He said, "You must be born again." It is a doorway that opens to any touch: we must ourselves only will to go through it. Have you never started to open a door, after you have rung a bell, only to find there was a hand opening the door to you from the other side—so that you both went in, and were welcomed in, at the same moment? The same thing happens spiritually. Christ never drives anyone in, we are free to enter or stay outside: but if we begin to enter, remembering that some things must be forever left outside when we enter that door, the Host is there to welcome us on the other side. I know people who have wished and even prayed for years that this great, liberating experience might be theirs. On closer questioning, one is likely to find that they (a) failed to isolate and specify the sins they were confessing, or the needs which they were bringing to Him, (b) took them back after nominally and emotionally surrendering them to Him (one must give up to Him in perfect trust, as one does to a doctor when going under an operation), (c) failed to let go of the will in a final, complete and irrevocable act, (d) did not pay the price of a continuing relation with Him, or (e) never got far enough to begin putting His power to work on concrete situations in their own or other people's lives. Where these steps are really taken, our experiment of faith is unfailingly met by His Presence and power.

This opens up the rich and fascinating realm of power-giving prayer. If people put as much time into prayer itself as they put into arguing about it with themselves or others, the world might be a very different place. For prayer produces power—ask anybody who prays! I have lately been discovering (what I theoretically knew, I suppose, but needed to know by the confirmation of experience), that the increment of power from prayer can almost be measured: I *know* that people, situations, my own spirit, are definitely affected by prayer. This must not be the tense prayer which is projected self-will: it must be the open prayer that catches the will and grace of God, as dry fields catch rain in summer; we need much receptive passivity, we need to bake and rest and stretch and relax and consider and decide in the love of God. Prayer is for the revealing and release of God's will, not for its improvement or alteration. Men in prayer do learn the will of God—not all of it, but as much as they need to know then to take the next step. When we come saying to God, "Lord, what wilt thou have me to do?" not in curiosity but in commitment—not in despair but in dedication—then we begin to know. To an eager, waiting, given human spirit, that loves God and His will, the Spirit makes His will known. For God's best gifts are not for the gifted, but for the *given.* Does prayer make people happy? Prayer reminds them of those things, the doing of which makes them happy. Prayer gets us into, or back into, the will of God, "whose service is perfect freedom" and perfect happiness.

One of the things which makes the spiritual experience seem difficult, and at times threatens it altogether with unreality, is what we call "ups and downs"—as the old Negro spiritual says, "Sometimes I'm up, sometimes I'm down." We must be prepared for cycles in spiritual experience, else there would be such monotony as would counteract growth. These cycles occur in life, as well as in people. Mr. H. W. Prentis, Jr., President of the Armstrong Cork Co., traces these general cycles as follows: we go from bondage to spiritual faith, from spiritual faith to courage, from courage to freedom, from freedom to some measure of physical abundance, from abundance to selfishness, from selfishness to complacency, from complacency to apathy, from apathy to fear, from fear to dependency, and from dependency back again to bondage. At any time, we may see some kinds of religion which are old and going to seed; and we may see other kinds that are laying hold again of the ageless power that comes from Christ, Who is like radium at the center of history. Chesterton says there was a time during the Dark Ages when the Church could not do much else but "go on stubbornly repeating the Creed." That is a very good thing to do, in the "down" period, when it comes: set your feet on the rock of what is objective and historic, not on the sands of your own emotions. Also, look for the meaning of the darkness through which you pass: God, if He did not send it, at least allowed it, so that you might learn something from it. And you will come out of the period of darkness, dryness, apathy, with something you did not have when you went into it. Those who say (1) that they never have these periods, or (2) that they know the full and final answer to them, are religious egotists who have never lived deeply.

But there is one fortification against needless sags and depressions in the spiritual life: and that is the cultivation of practical and systematic spiritual habits. In all times of the Christian era, people have found it useful to do the following things:

1. Study the Bible. Here is the double record of God's search for man and man's search for God. It is a plain-spoken old Book, with unvarnished sinners and back-sliding saints in it from cover to cover. Its peaks of spiritual insight and experience have never been surpassed, but it makes no excuse for human weakness nor attempt to hide it. We keep reading it, because in it we keep seeing ourselves. The times, the clothes, the customs change: the people, the situations, human nature—not much! In the Psalms, for instance, you will find just about every mood that man can feel—exalted, rebellious, unselfish, forgotten, devout, cynical, tender, cruel. The words themselves are like drains in a wound; they canalize for us the emotions which, without them, could hardly find such full expression. Here is no serene book of pleasant affirma-

tions: the peak of the Old Testament is the looking for a Suffering Servant, and the peak of the New Testament is the Suffering Servant Himself, living as the lowliest among the lowly, and crucified on a Cross. Strange how in Him people have found the deepest peace and joy this world has ever known! The more our minds feed in this rich pasture, the stronger will our spirits be. How many young people who do not go the way of the world but keep strong in the right way, and how many old people who do not become old in spirit but live always with "light at evening time,"[5] how many sufferers who have no bitterness, and servants of mankind who know no discouragement, find their unfailing source of inspiration in this Book—"the Book," as many who love it most are fond of calling it. A good text, a concordance to find your way by, and a commentary to help you to understand—these will help you to make the study of the Bible a spiritual habit for life.

2. Pray. Fix a time for it each day, and keep to it no matter what happens. Get alone and quiet if possible. First shut out the world from your consciousness, so that you can get quiet before God—this is the meaning of closing one's eyes, kneeling down in a private and familiar place. Let your thoughts settle down, as leaves in a whirlwind slowly settle to the ground. Then the mind is lifted up, by our wills and also by the drawing power of Him Whom we seek. Then begins to

[5] Zechariah 14:7.

pour out the confession, the thanksgiving, the petition, the intercession, which expresses our need and desire. If we would truly pray, we must remember Dr. Glenn Clark's thought, that prayer means yearning plus relinquishment: we offer the best desiring of our hearts, then we leave it all to God asking only that His best will be done. There will be periods of uneventfulness in prayer, as in all deep relationships even with other people: but as one is both self-giving and receptive, there comes the moment when event takes place—there is an increment of power, of peace, of enlightenment, of healing, of assurance that prayer is being answered. Beside the fixed times for prayer, morning and evening, let us learn the simple art of being in touch with God at all times—as we walk, or work, or play, or visit with people—keeping, as it were, one ear open to Him all the time, whatever we are doing, so that we may not miss the fresh inspiration from Him that will heighten it. George Müller was a great "doer," whose work cared for thousands of orphans in England: but he said once, "I see more clearly than ever that the first and primary business, to which I ought to attend every day, is to have my soul happy in the Lord." This was the secret of his long, effective service: if so busy a man thought it essential to take time to pray, what excuse is there for our little lives, so often cluttered rather than truly busy, to neglect it?

3. Go to your church. Church-going, it seems to me, is two things: it is an indication of direction and inten-

tion; and it is a chance for fresh contact with the Source of happiness. Many who stay away from church do so on the grounds that they are "just as good" as those who go. This constitutes a double misunderstanding: one, those who go to church do not usually go because they are satisfied with themselves, but precisely because they are not; and two, it does not reveal a very high order of humility to think you are "just as good" as somebody else—in fact, if you consult the famous parable of the Publican and the Pharisee, you will find the Master was harder on the man who thought well of himself than on the man who felt dissatisfied with himself! There are some things you can only get in church—not even over the radio listening to a service: one of them is Holy Communion, the thankful remembrance of the sacrifice of Jesus Christ, His broken Body symbolized in the broken Bread and outpoured Wine, which is one of the very greatest means by which He continues to touch and strengthen His people. Another is corporate and united worship with other people, where one is aware that he is a member of the human family, and one of the called-out family of God: each helps and is helped by the others. We have something else to do in the world beside cultivate our own souls; we are set to make conquest of the evil in the world, and build the Kingdom of God in the hearts of men. Does anybody believe you can do this through a large number of individual sharpshooters, each one fighting the war in his own way? As Dr. Elton Trueblood says, "For faith to become concrete it must be embodied in a human society. Separated, individual believers will not be able to make any headway against the present storm."[6] Every living church should have within it smaller cells for spiritual development, in which seekers and all others may find spiritual fellowship and training.

Now let me tell you of one woman who found the "greatest source of happiness," when she thought all happiness was gone from her for life.

She is past middle-age, and a person of obvious cultivation and refinement. But the way she was thinking of herself was evident in her manner of speaking, as well as in some indefinable slouching of the shoulders one often notices in people who think ill of themselves. She apologized for coming, said there was probably nothing that could be done—her professional work was growing impossible through her deafness, she would not ask her friends for help, she desperately needed congenial work. She had had plenty of Spiritual Exposure, and said that lines of old hymns kept coming into her mind, haunting her with the need for a greater consecration than she thought she could give. And she had done a good deal of spiritual reading. I listened, but conversation was difficult because of her extreme deafness. I got up and went to the desk, when she had finished her story,

[6] *The Predicament of Modern Man,* p. 71.

and wrote down a kind of prescription for her: it began as follows:

"I think you need God and faith more than a job. 'Seek ye first . . .' *Then* the job."

I then introduced her to a friend of mine who is also very deaf, but spiritually released about it: they were not far from the same age, and talked long *and loud* to each other. They met more than once. This second woman introduced her to other friends who included her, for she needed human companionship. She went out with a smile, and that hang-dog look gone from those shoulders as well as from her face. She came to meetings and picked up all she could from atmosphere, and some things were repeated to her later. A card from her says, "I have had a most happy vacation. I am so much more cheerful and social, my friends speak of it. I guess it is due to the awakening I have had. I am so grateful, and hope I may pass some of it on to other people. I certainly am getting a lot more out of life than I did."

It is a glorious thing to see an experience like that take place over the course of a few weeks. You realize how many people could be happy who are not, if only they found the great Source of happiness! And they can find it. It makes you see clearly the great truth of Dr. Leslie Weatherhead's remark, "The opposite of joy is not sorrow. It is unbelief."[7]

[7] *This Is the Victory,* p. 171.

V

Understanding Ourselves

MANY unhappy people do not understand themselves, while those who have found happiness (principally in spiritual faith) are mature enough to understand themselves and so realize their own part in creating the happiness or unhappiness of their lives.

Why is it, do you suppose, that religion helps people to see themselves honestly? Well, I think this is the reason. If God is not very real to us, we become ourselves the final arbiters of our own lives: we might say that in direct proportion as the reality of God fades out of a human life, his own ego takes the central place in his life. Of course other people and the world at large matter; but we are talking of something very personal and inward, way down where, as someone said, "we dwell alone with our willingnesses and our unwillingnesses." God is the one big check on human egotism—other egos are not enough—we fight them with impunity—but when we fight God we discover we are fighting our best, i.e., our real, selves. As a daily working proposition, perhaps the only thing great enough to stand in the road of the onrushing ego is the sense of accountability to a Divine Being, now and hereafter. The less God is real, the more I become god to myself, or else seek to find some human authority whom I tend to deify in order to give me faith.

It is true, of course, that not all religious pople are happy. How do you account for this? First, a good many neurotics turn to religion for comfort and do not find it, because they need personal counseling of a medical, psychiatric or spiritual kind, and will not be able to draw from "religion in general" the special help they need. Second, of those who seek religion in the ordinary way, there are literally thousands who never get through to the place where they understand what it means to be a Christian. They may begin with little capacity for self-analysis, or so great a "healthy-mindedness" that they do not tend to think much about their faults: such people will go on more and more identifying their present condition with the accepted aims of the religion they profess, and wind up complacent Pharisees without knowing they are doing it! The harm to their own souls, the damage done in driving away from religion those with enough psychological insight or natural humility to recognize that, whatever Christianity is, this is *not* Christianity, is immeasurable. If you call yourself a spiritual person, and are reading this passage without a twinge that says, "Is that I?" you are perilously close to what I am describing! Pascal once said, "There are only two kinds of men, the righteous who believe themselves sinners: the rest, sinners, who believe themselves righteous."[1] And C. S. Lewis says, "When a man is getting better he understands more and more clearly the evil that is still left in him. When a man is getting worse, he understands his own badness less and less. A moderately bad man knows he's not very good: a thoroughly bad man thinks he's all right."[2] Trust Gamaliel Bradford, that inveterate understander of the human heart, to dig up a revealing passage somewhere about self-satisfaction: can you beat this one from the pen of Dumas, who is speaking of himself? "When the hand of the Lord closes the two horizons of my life, letting fall the veil of his love between the nothingness that precedes and the nothingness that follows the life of man, he may examine the intermediate space with his most rigorous scrutiny, he will find there not one single evil thought or one action for which I feel that I should reproach myself."[3] What must a man who could write that have been like in the ordinary rubs and frictions of daily life, so seldom entirely one-sided in their origin? We smile at such unblushing complacency and self-satisfaction: but do we smile when we ask how often it has been characteristic of ourselves?

The very chief characteristic of real Christianity in people is their constant awareness that they fall daily

[1] Quoted Niebuhr, *The Nature and Destiny of Man,* p. 257.
[2] *Christian Behaviour,* p. 25.
[3] *A Naturalist of Souls,* p. 196.

into sin. When they form judgments of the conduct of others, these are characterized by a compassion and an understanding which proceeds from the fact that they realize they themselves have done or might have done, or might some time do, this same thing: it does not alter the clarity of the moral assessment, but it profoundly alters the amount of self-righteousness that stands behind the judgment. "There is no level of achievement," writes Reinhold Niebuhr, "upon which man can have or actually has an easy conscience."[4] No one can be a real Christian without a constant sense of fault and sin, and at the same time of God's forgiveness and love if we are honest and penitent about the wrong. This paradox, this double consciousness, lies at the very heart of the Christian faith. It is not an "up-and-down" in succession: it is an "up-and-down" simultaneously. We are "up" always because we are God's redeemed and forgiven children: we are "down" always because we are continually slipping away from Him and His will into courses that wind up in pride or despair. Evil never lets us alone: it attacks, not where we know we are weak only, but where we think we are strong. If you vaguely know something is the matter, and cannot put your finger on just what it is, look for a fault right where you are sure you possess a virtue! Positive virtues so easily turn into pride, and self-effacing ones into self-pity! We need not think we are Christians unless we feel deep in our bones that, but for God, we

[4] *The Nature and Destiny of Man,* p. 131.

are hopeless: nor are we Christians if we feel continually (since God exists) that we are hopeless.

Most people simply do not understand themselves, nor know what drives them. A methodical woman who does her housework and routine with the greatest regularity and responsibility may be a trial to her house-hold because she is so inflexible about her schedule: she may be what the psychologists call a "rigid normal"—and a too rigid normal is very close to being abnormal! A man who is generous with his money to his family and community needs may flatter himself, as he will often be flattered by others: he may be sublimely unaware that he gives all this and is generous to others as a way of buying off his conscience for being also very generous to himself. Most good and decent people never get any corrective after they cease to be children: if one of the family attempts it, the come-back is, "Well, look at this and this which *you* do—you're not so hot yourself," as if fault in another excused it in ourselves!—as if sin in you canceled out the truth of what you may tell me about myself, seeing me, as you probably do, much clearer than I see myself!

We ought to strive to be open to the insights which the opinions of others may give us concerning ourselves. Others see us much as we are, have no fear about that! Nine-tenths of them will analyze us with appalling accuracy in talking with a third person. It is considered "manners" not to mention these things to the person most concerned, though the mention of them might save this person and others untold suffering. But now and then someone has the courage and true friendship to say a direct word to us about one of our faults. It may be said smilingly, it may be said tentatively, because this person is feeling his way with us, and does not wish unnecessarily to rouse our antagonism. It may be said in the heat of temper or resentment, when it is less likely to gain access to our attention. But, however it comes, and whether from someone we know as a true friend, or someone we think a little impertinent for speaking this way, whether it comes from someone younger than we or someone we think is "in no position" to speak to us in this fashion, this is one of the real crises and turning-places of our lives. If we throw it back upon what we call the immaturity, or bad manners, or criticalness, of the other person, and do not heed it, a great opportunity has been lost. If we accept it, are ready to talk it over, and honestly seek to get to the bottom of it, we are likely to take a significant step ahead. The probable truth is that, however blunt or even brutal the words of another may sound to us, they are not blunt nor brutal enough to fit the case, and there is more of fault in us than they have any idea of, more inward self-justification and complacency than they have even implied. For most of us have but one positive source of satisfaction, and it is what we are pleased to call our "clean consciences." This is our most fruitful source of pride and moral stagnancy. As an old colored man with wisdom said, "If you b'lieve you're where you're gwine, you ain't gwine to go!"

It is a desperately hard thing to face ourselves. It is difficult, first, to find a simple criterion, into which we can look as into a mirror and see what really goes on in the hearts of us. It is difficult, second, to find another person with whom we can talk, and who will not either demolish us by destructive criticism, or let us off too lightly by chiming in with our own ready egotism and its white-washing process. But it is also difficult because our egos resist change more than anything else in the world. We often want to change other people, or circumstances—we even wish our own natures were changed, but that is a very different thing from doing anything about getting them changed, or even taking one definite step in that direction. Why do we resist change so? Because it really seems to us that the only thing left to our self-respect, indeed the only thing left of a real self at all, is these rags of accomplishment, complacency and self-satisfaction—if these went, we'd be reduced to a grease-spot! I can well remember a time in my life, long after my first decisive spiritual experience, when I was facing the need to take another big step forward. I could almost see my *self* shrinking out of sight under the withering effects of an honest facing of my faults, and, like Alice in Wonderland when she was shrinking, I wondered whether I wouldn't go out like a light if this process went on! But this was not the real case: when I let go deeply inside, my true "self" was never more fulfilled and expressed, and I realized that all this fanfare of resistance and self-will is the protective device of the ego to keep the true "self" from emerging and being victorious. This fear of giving up, of giving in, is a contrivance of the ego. As Fénelon said, "If we looked carefully into ourselves, we should find some secret place where we hide what we think we are not obliged to sacrifice to God."[5] But until that false ego dies, the true self cannot live. And the death of an ego is the greatest of all human crises.

We must go further with this to understand it. We are meant to be "selves." The true self is to the soul what the body is to the life: in this world they are inseparable. So long as it is right to live, so long as we are not funking a challenge to lay down our lives for a cause that needs us (as millions of men did in the war, as Woodrow Wilson did for the League of Nations), it is right to seek not only to maintain, but to develop our real selves. There are people who, looking into the Christian way of life from outside, think that it means a kind of sacrifice which even Jesus Himself did not practice. There were hungry people about Him, yet He ate enough to keep alive: cold people, but He wore enough to preserve His life and health: needy people, yet He slept enough to maintain His strength. We are not only permitted, we are obligated,

[5] *Selections from Fénelon,* Follen, p. 268.

as Christians to train our minds, to develop our social relations, to become just as much of a person as we are capable of being. But there is a great difference between a person who sets out to do this in his own strength and for his own rewards or satisfaction, and a person who realizes that this development of the self must be a God-given thing to be used for the benefit of other people. The false ego and the true self are always getting mixed in our minds. The true self comes up to a situation and begins to meet it calmly, courageously, adequately: but then the false ego comes piling in, right through the channel of the true self, and begins to deal with it impatiently, fearingly and inadequately. The ego dies, like a cat with nine lives, beginning with one great blow which takes place when the self accepts the will and sovereignty of God, but we must beat it again and again with many blows till it is really dead, then the true self, the real self, the self God intended when He created us, rises to the top and on the whole (one must say this, for the perfect completion of the process does not take place in this life) the real, true self is in the saddle.

Stop for a moment and realize that you have a "real, true self." Part of the struggle of your life is to let that true self emerge and find scope. We can be so preoccupied with the ego, with the false aspects of ourselves, that we never enjoy any hope of being our real and true selves. Moreover, we often so misunderstand the Christian faith that we think it means the complete ignoring, and the constant disapproval, of ourselves. In one aspect, this is true. But when Jesus said, "Thou shalt love thy neighbour as thyself," He certainly accepted a degree of self-love. He assumed such care for oneself as, for instance, the industry that pays our way in the world. That He called, and still calls, some men and women to go out on faith and throw themselves upon the mercies of a humanity whom they selflessly serve, does not mean that He intended or recommended such a procedure for all. It is right that we should be interested in the work which absorbs these selves of ours, in such development of ourselves as makes of us the best servants of God and mankind that we can be, in any talent, study, or even possession or appearance, that can forward this end. Such things are to be regarded as gifts from God, and to be used unselfishly, not for our own advancement. Self-hatred, self-depreciation, are not in His plan or scheme. When God has lifted us up from the valley of despair, self-judgment, whither our disenchantment about ourselves had banished us, He gives to us the derived but conscious dignity that belongs to the children of God. To the end of the chapter, we shall be drawn backwards by our failures and faults; but there is a regality to all who live the Christian life, of whom St. Paul said proudly, "Ye serve the Lord Christ." If you take the Christian way and accept the Christian forgiveness, put away from you forever the hang-dog, woe-begone emotion about yourself. Know that you are God's child. Develop every capacity God has hidden within you. Become as much of a person as you can. In this sense, love yourself—and then you will be in far better position to love your neighbour.

Now much of this battle between the ego and the self takes place in the subliminal self, in the subconscious. Whatever you call it, it means the storehouse of the mind in which the images, remembrance, emotions of past experience are kept with almost the accuracy of a filing system. The cooperativeness and accessibility of this storehouse of experience seems in direct proportion to the freedom from conflict in the whole personality. I have seen a man speaking in public into whose conscious mind there seemed to keep welling up out of this forgotten treasury of experience fresh illustrations and illuminating and unexpected ideas: they came so freely and with such aptness that you could see them delight the speaker himself as they "came through," as if he were watching the process like a spectator. I said to myself, "There is a man whose conversion has extended well into his subconscious." Dr. Fritz Kunkel says, "There are hidden energies in the deeper layers of the human mind which may give a terrific power to those who could evoke them."[6] On the other hand, conflict freezes this flow between the conscious and unconscious self. When the basic forces of the self are pulling against each other, there is a stoppage, as if conflict were able

[6] *In Search of Maturity*, p. 20.

to batten down these hidden but powerful forces and keep us from using them. Forgetfulness, inattention (which might often be spelled "inner tension"), self-consciousness, saying the opposite of what we mean, are signs of disorder in the relations between the conscious and subliminal self. Moreover, the powers of these "deeper, unconscious layers" are instinctive, and have in them much that would shame us if they came to the surface: we must therefore keep feeding down into the subconscious the kind of thoughts, convictions, emotions that strengthen the good and positive, and allay the force of the evil and negative. To quote Dr. Kunkel again, "We are more at the mercy of the dark powers than we know. Every one, even the coolest and calmest moralist, is their slave. And to master consciously our unconscious forces is the only way which can help us to replace our bloody, so-called civilization by real culture."[7]

This leads us to consider conflict. As all life is movement and we can never stand still, we expect the steady necessity for new decisions to be made in the face of new situations. We must weigh one thing against another. If one is reasonably well and rested and untroubled, this does not tax him unduly: but if he be fatigued and sick in body or mind, it may put him "in conflict." Now we need to remember that there will always exist some tensions in personality, because they exist always in life. The conflicts between progress

[7] *Ibid.*, p. 58.

and conservatism, body and spirit, self and society, the ideal and the real, the absolute and compromise, youth and age, reason and emotion, are abiding conflicts: our growth in character depends on how we meet them and what we do with them. We must make these creative, not distinctive, conflicts. When these tensions in life produce tensions in us that go beyond the ordinary, they tend to become neurotic. Many of them can be caught and dealt with before they reach this stage, many can be caught after they have reached it. As Dr. Karen Horney reminds us, "The more we realize what infinite harm neurotic conflicts inflict on the personality, the more stringent appears the need truly to resolve them. But since . . . this cannot be done by rational decision nor by evasion nor by the exertion of will power, how can it be done? There is only one way: the conflicts can be resolved only by changing those conditions within the personality that brought them into being."[8]

What we look for, plainly, is the release of our emotions. Our emotions are meant to be enjoyable to us and to others. To be this, they must be so far as possible undivided, and come up out of an integrated self. We often see today the absence of adequate emotion, or the presence of exaggerated amounts of it. People in conflict, people whose subconscious is cut off from cooperation with their conscious selves by unresolved conflict, cannot release their true feelings. And because

[8] *Our Inner Conflicts,* p. 217.

the emotions are frozen, the thoughts are frozen, too, —as a child in school may do poorly in an examination, not because he does not know the answers, but because his thought-process is choked off by the emotion of fear. Much social intercourse is made stiff and miserable by an emotional stoppage in people. We quote Dr. Horney again, "The most comprehensive formulation of the therapeutic goals is the striving for *wholeheartedness*: to be without pretense, to be emotionally sincere, to be able to put the whole of oneself into one's feelings, one's work, one's beliefs. It can be approximated only to the extent that conflicts are resolved."[9]

A great deal of conflict arises in the failure to discover a synthesis between the freedom of emotional release, and the observance of conformity to moral ideals. It looks as if release would come by giving free rein to the emotions that have long been damned up: and as if adherence to moral standards were tantamount to "repression." But things are not so simple as this. For the breach of ideals in which we truly believe sets up another conflict not to be ignored: we must find a "both . . . and" here and not look for an "either . . . or." This dilemma is due to a false understanding of certain psychological beliefs, and a failure to realize that psychology itself is continually revising its judgments. Again Dr. Horney gives us great help: "In the analytical situation Freud's discarding of moral values

[9] *Ibid.*, p. 242.

—a consequence of his viewing psychology as a natural science—has contributed toward making the analyst just as blind as the patient to contradictions of this sort. The analyst thinks it 'unscientific' to have moral values of his own or to take any interest in those of the patient."[10] And Dr. Kunkel gives a strong warning to those who accept the religious view-point, yet look to scientific psychology to deal with all matters: "People with character difficulties, moral deviations and vices, are sent to doctors as though they were sick. The physical and mental diseases certainly belong to the realm of medicine, and therefore the ethical evaluation in these cases must be avoided. But if vices are diseases, they cease to be vices; and theology, sending the drunkard and the gambler to the physician, relinquishes its last connection with reality: the ethical task."[11] He is right about the common tendency of clergymen, for instance, to come up against a problem that derives from some aberration in character, and to consider themselves unable to deal with it, and who therefore send the person in need to a psychiatrist. Where there are signs of sickness, this is the proper course: few clergy know enough psychiatry to practise it without constant checking with a trained scientist. But there are clearly two sides even to mental sickness: there is the situation, which may need to be dealt with by one who knows the psychological science; but

10 *Our Inner Conflicts,* p. 134.
11 *In Search of Maturity,* p. 17.

there are also the "conditions within the personality that brought (the conflicts) into being."[12] Who, what, shall undertake, not alone the healing of a particular neurosis, or psychosis (if it can be reached and cured), but the re-making of a personality, the implanting of a sound and enduring set of standards, the setting of the life upon a new path of progress toward happiness? Here is wanted some synthesis which draws together not alone the scattered fragments of personality, but gives the person a new relation to the very universe in which he lives. This can only come as he comes by some living faith that lifts him above himself, sets him in relation to his fellows on a new basis, and makes him feel at home in the universe. To understand ourselves, we must know how to adjust the many sides of ourselves to each other, to adjust ourselves to others, and to adjust ourselves to life as life is and not as we may wish it were or may have decided to think that it is because we should like to have it so.

There is an old Arabic legend, little known in the western world, to the effect that when Adam and Eve were driven out of the Garden of Eden, the angel who held the flaming sword said to them, "Henceforth your hearts must be your paradise." Well, it would have been true *in* the Garden of Eden if they had stayed there long enough, i.e., if they were the parents of the human nature which we know. For the happiness of Paradise never rests permanently in any cir-

[12] See page 98.

cumstance or given condition: it lies in our own hearts' reaction to those outward situations. As more and more we understand a world that was not created to be our play-pen or our oyster, but our training ground and schooling-place for becoming such persons as we were given life to become—as more and more we realize that "the way of man is not in himself: it is not in man that walketh to direct his steps,"[13] and that God is the X in the equation of life, without which the answer cannot be found—we shall begin to discover how we can find happiness. If we are to find it, and if it is not to be either cheap or temporary, we must learn a great many things which it will take time and study to know. The best way to learn those truths and values, those ideals and standards, those habits and spiritual practises, is to be brought up from childhood in the Christian faith. But for those who have not enjoyed that privilege, they can be learned the longer, harder way. And for those whose lack of moral and spiritual foundations has carried them far afield, so that their lives are now a tangled snarl, and who seem even to themselves beyond the place where they can ever find happiness, let me remind them of Amiel's profound saying, "The redeemed are happier than the elect." No one appreciates the final spiritual liberation so much as one who has long been imprisoned in defeat and despair, and finally finds his freedom.

To sum up, then, to understand ourselves we need

[13] Jeremiah 10:23.

a great "Other" in Whom we see ourselves and especially our defects; we need a constant consciousness of those defects which shall be for us not matter for discouragement but for growth; we need to see the faults which lurk in the middle of virtues; we must be open to the insights which other people help us to possess as regards our real character; we need to find the power that is released when our subconscious selves work in cooperation with our conscious intentions in true emotional freedom; we must keep clear as to whether our need is moral and to be dealt with by faith, or a sickness which needs expert medical or psychiatric attention.

I close with a quieting, stimulating passage from Kierkegaard: "Everyone for himself, in quiet inwardness before God, shall humble himself before what it means in the strictest sense to be a Christian, admit candidly before God how it stands with him, so that he might yet accept the grace which is offered to everyone that is imperfect, that is, to everyone. And then, no further; then for the rest let him attend to his work, be glad in it, love his wife, be glad in her, bring up his children with joyfulness, love his fellow men, rejoice in life. If anything further is required, God will surely let him understand, and in such case will also help him further. . . ."[14]

[14] *Training in Christianity,* translated by Walter Lowrie, p. 71.

VI

Dealing with Trouble

MANY people can maintain a fair degree of happiness in life, until the day of trouble comes. And then because theirs has really been a fair-weather happiness, it departs from them. They can stand most of the long stretches, with some boredom and some heart-ache in them: but then comes the dreadful news that someone they love has been killed in an accident, or the doctor who has been non-committal says it is "malignant," or the savings are swept away at a stroke, or a rift with a loved one develops into a permanent breach. No one greets these things with equanimity unless he has schooled himself in a hard unfeelingness; the heart beats faster, the blood pressure goes up or down as the case may be; there is some suffering that ensues. If we are to possess real and abiding happiness, it must be something that can see its way through all these things, and yet remain greater than they. You can't be happy until you can look all existence fair in the face—death, suffering, evil, pain—and know that there is an answer for it. The consciousness, sometimes sharp, sometimes dim, that one's happiness (or faith) is not enough to sustain us should one of these things come to us or someone we love, may be a life-long anxiety to us.

We must make a distinction between real trouble, and what Dr. Kunkel calls "normal crisis." There is a kind of person that is always "feeling funny" in the heart or stomach or head, which is a way of gaining attention. There are problems to be met, decisions to be made, situations to work out, for everyone. If these cause restlessness, fatigue, a desire to run away into drink or sex or some other escape, if we weep a little, and tell the walls of the bathroom how unjust we think life to be, this is no great matter. As Dr. Kunkel says, such things "are, in countless cases, the adequate expression for the normal crisis, as it happens and should happen in every human life."[1]

There are three things we should all like to do with trouble: avoid it, explain it, and meet it if it comes. We cannot avoid it for very long, for life is not constituted in that way.

Is there any explanation of trouble? It is part of the whole problem of evil in the world; and no one has ever wholly solved the mystery of evil in the world of a good God. But there are some considerations that have greatly helped people to keep their faith in God, and their happiness in life, in spite of the presence of evil. One of them is that if man is meant to develop character, to grow, he must do it by making decisions, decisions which must be free if they are to have moral

[1] *In Search of Maturity,* Fritz Kunkel, p. 9.

significance. Therefore at creation God must endow man with freedom—that is the inwardness of the Garden of Eden story. Now if God placed real freedom in the hands of man, man must be really able to use that freedom according to his own desire. There must be a choice, between a better and worse, between a good and bad, if this freedom is to be more than merely nominal. Man was given freedom and man misused it. There is evil in the world because no such thing as growth or character would be possible in a world already perfect. God's creation is not a state of perfection, but a march toward it. As John Stuart Mill suggestively wrote in a letter to a friend, "It would be a great moral improvement to most persons . . . if they firmly believe the world to be under the government of a Being who, willing only good, leaves evil in the world solely in order to stimulate human faculties by an unremitting struggle against every form of it." The universe itself seems on the side of good in this struggle: this is reflected in man's readiness to make permanent (so far as he can) what is good, and to be done (as soon as possible) with what works against his long-range interests. Take, for example, democracy: it is the longest-standing form of government in some of the great nations, and none of them that enjoy it want to discard it. But the dictatorships—how long do they last? They grind their iron heel into their people's necks and from the beginning there are those who seek its uprooting: their number grows until this is accomplished. There is, I think, a very fruitful suggestion in a sentence of the late William Temple: "Evil has at least this much of good about it that its own nature renders it self-destructive."[2]

Christianity has never sought nor claimed to have a final answer about why evil is in the world. Two convictions it has held from the first. One is that our proper attitude toward evil is not to seek to understand why it is here, but to deal with it effectively with a view to overcoming it. The Pharisees, and even Jesus' own disciples, on meeting a blind man, sought to answer the question why he was born blind—was it due to sin in himself or his parents?[3] Jesus took a strictly practical view of the matter, saying, "Neither hath this man sinned, nor his parents: but that the works of God should be made manifest in him." The other Christian conviction about evil is that, while its nature often cannot be changed, its effect can be changed, and its total influence therefore transmuted into a kind of good. Jesus did this supremely with His own cross. And all who meet their own personal crosses in real faith and victory follow after Him in spirit. That is why one can never evaluate an event or experience as "evil": he must see what he can make of it first, and only then evaluate it. Its evaluation depends upon his nature as well as upon the nature of the event. Emerson spoke once of "accepting our

[2] *The Church Looks Forward,* p. 183.
[3] St. John, chapter nine.

actual companions and circumstances, however humble or odious, as the mystic officials to whom the universe has delegated its whole pleasure for us."[4] This is not to say that evil is not evil: moral wrong is always moral wrong—but the way we take moral wrong done against us, for example, may have in it very much of moral good. Part of the experience and adventure of living life with faith in one's heart is seeing where and how what appears to be tragedy can be turned into at least a measure of triumph.

So we find a law which we can set down simply in this way: *it is not what happens to us, but how we take it, that matters*. I knew two women who found themselves in identical situations. They were each childless and well-to-do, and each lost her husband in early middle age. One of them was of a naturally retiring disposition, but she made up her mind she would live her life usefully: she found places to take responsibility, developed leadership, and became a very outstanding citizen in her community. The other was naturally of an outgoing nature, with much to give to people; but she drew into the shell of her grief, lived in the past, and slowly committed suicide by self-pity. The difference between them lay, not in the circumstances, but in what they did with the circumstances.

An illness, especially of a long duration and uncertain outcome, can seem to put an end to happiness in life. But again, it all depends on what you do with it.

4 Essay on "Experience."

A clergyman friend of mine, at the very height of his powers, was laid low for two years with tuberculosis. His body had to go out of action, but his spirit did not go out of action. Quietly he bided God's time, and God raised him up to his work again. Speaking of this in a group recently he said, "A good case of sickness is better than a college education." He had used that time apart to develop the interior life. Some of us are more carried along by our own activity, while we think it is faith that is upholding us, than we like to admit: it may take an enforced idleness to show us that as man does not live by bread alone, neither does he live by activity alone. It is a lesson badly needed to be learned by our generation. An elderly woman was knocked down when a balloon tire flew off a passing truck: her hip was broken, and her active life came to an end. I went to the hospital to see her as soon as possible, and she looked up out of great pain with a wonderful smile and said, "Well, I wonder what God has for us to do here!" And at once she began spreading about her the joyous, victorious Christian faith that was hers. And *that* part of her active life went on. I hear someone say: "But why do these things happen to God's saints?" And I reply, "I do not know. I know that faith is no guarantee against trouble, but only against defeat. I know that it is possible to meet every situation with victory and with faith, and that is Christianity's answer to those troubles which come upon all alike." John Wesley had a sister, Patty, who married a brute of a man named Westley Hall, and suffered all her life with him: she said once, "Evil was not kept from me, but evil has been kept from hurting me."[5]

What, then, shall we do when trouble strikes?

We should first, I think, have anticipated it. By this I do not mean brooding over things that may happen, but rather realizing that we are alive in the world that *is*, not the world of fancy, and we are not life's darlings and so may expect the normal amount of trouble. Many a family during the war never took it in that men were being killed, till one of their own boys was killed: they saw the casualty lists, they heard of neighbours' sons who had been lost; but they never let the thing touch them, never felt really a part of this world as it is, persisted in a feeling that somehow they would be kept exempt from it all. When one has done this, one is not only incapable of giving true sympathy to anyone else, but one is utterly unready when the blow falls. Work out your philosophy before the thing happens; for when it happens you will not be able to do it. It is a bad thing to brood about uncertainties in the future, and possible tragedies, some of which never come to pass. But now and then to give a nod of recognition to the Grim Reaper, and to realize that someone lying in pain on a hospital bed might have been ourselves—that is a salutary exercise. We ought not to come away from such considerations

5 *Wesley and His Century,* W. H. Fitchett, p. 30.

with an easy feeling that we are "lucky": we ought to come away more than ever identified with the sufferings of others, more than ever aware of the real world in which we live, farther and farther removed from the blind, wishful thinking which is the characteristic outlook of so many of us. Anything can happen to anybody. Therefore, while we may be saddened, we should never quite be shocked or surprised. But this can only be avoided by reasonable anticipation.

The next thing we need to do, always, is to face fully the fact of the trouble. Again, I do not mean always anticipating the worst, as many do when someone falls ill, and they surround him with negative and fear-ridden emotions and thoughts. But I mean looking the indisputable facts square in the face. A man whose legs are paralyzed must face his physical limitations: but I know one who has done this, yet carried on from his room a considerable business. A weak heart means greater care than most people require, and imposes some limitations, though the longevity of people with "heart disease" is proverbial. Let us not push the facts from us, nor engage in too much wishful thinking. Astonishing cures sometimes are effected, and we must not fail to allow for them: but sometimes they are not forth-coming, and we must make up our minds to it that the situation is just what it is, not what we wish it were. Great unhappiness can ensue unless we have a ready machinery in our minds and emotions for the acceptance of realities. I suggest it is well to put it down for a fact, hand it over to God and our own subconscious to deal with, and then turn soon to duties and other thoughts: to this end our lives should be well stocked with interests, concerns and friends. Betsey Barton, in that remarkable chronicle of courage *And Now to Live Again* says, "When we have faced our hurt, when we have faced it fully and all its consequences, and when we have learned to deal with it in all times and in all ways, then and then only can it be said that reeducation has begun."

I think a third thing we need to do is to get all the goodness out of the trouble. This means not resisting it too much. It means letting sorrow be sorrow, and giving rein to grief. If tears and strong crying are the natural vent, open it wide, do not choke it off in a false, Stoic courage. Many seek to go through trouble like someone flying through the cold upper ether, all bundled up so as to feel it as little as possible. Such people waste their suffering, it does nothing for them. They do not come out of it purged, humbled, made tender, strengthened, as they might. Many are afraid to "break down," to show their emotion, to give in to all they feel. But psychology well knows that such people are more likely to break later. There are times and situations which we simply have to live through. Even when we know the answer and the way to victory, we do not always manage to coordinate what we know with what we are experiencing. Let the shadows of those hours have their influence upon us: we were not meant to be just the same after this happened, as we were before. It is very good for some of us to find we are not as strong, as self-reliant, as indomitable, as we thought we were. It will be an experience well suffered if we come out of it more aware of our dependence on God and other people, less sure we can successfully manage our own lives.

A fourth help in trouble is to talk with other people. Rehearse the story with them, they will understand, and the voicing of it (provided it does not become a selfish indulgence for you) will give you help. Where people keep a combination of sympathy and strength, you will draw on both in them. Some things that people say and do, with the best intentions in the world, do not hit the mark: others hit it perfectly. It is the same with letters. But we should go on saying the best things we can, and writing them, for more people are hurt by our not saying what is in our hearts, and so entering into their situation, than we have any idea of. When our trouble involves a tangle of emotions, we often need tremendously a third person to help straighten us out. A young veteran, off on his own for years, came back to a greatly loved wife who had also been off on her own for the same number of years, in spite of the care of a child. They faced the usual housing difficulty and were cooped into a terribly small apartment. Two strong-willed individuals found the adjustment almost impossible to make. They were about to separate and call it a day, but decided to talk with an older friend who knew them well and loved them. This led to their seeing the picture more clearly, more emphasis upon *my* faults than upon the other person's and a reconciliation.

There is a fifth consideration here. Trouble may be a guide-post that indicates a change of place or occupation. We must be open to this. We do not trust God really unless we trust Him everywhere, and believe that He can and does over-rule in all situations. Even if this involves the loss of something we dearly wanted, it may mean our larger service in the end. A striking illustration of this is Samuel F. B. Morse. He was one of the best portrait painters of his time, and a man of varied interests and talents. Crossing the sea in 1832, he was discussing with another man the new marvels of electricity and the electro-magnet. He saw in a flash that messages might be sent by electric wires to distant points with lightning speed. He went to work on this and day after day he pondered and planned, setting up his apparatus at New York University where he was professor of art. About this time there came to him one of the greatest disappointments of his life. Through the vindictiveness of one man he was refused a commission to paint one of the rotunda panels in the Capitol at Washington. This bitter injustice ended his career as an artist: but it meant his complete dedication to the invention of the telegraph. Had he gone on his way as a successful artist, this might never have happened. He might have been less hurt; but the world would have lost a priceless contribution to progress.

But in the end, and when all is done, the great thing when trouble comes is to reach for your faith, and know where it is, so it can go to work quickly. When you fumble for medicine in the dark at night, you may drink iodine instead of aromatic spirits of ammonia: but when you know where to reach for it, you have it when you need it. Many of us, when trouble comes, are just like people looking for medicine in the dark—they do not know where to find it. How different a friend of mine who is a minister! One Sunday evening he preached a sermon to his people on the verse, "All things work together for good to them that love God." Afterwards one of his laymen said to him, "Dominie, you meant that for us—you wouldn't really expect to live up to that if anything happened to you, would you?" "Yes," said the minister, "I should expect it to apply in my own life, no matter what happened." On Tuesday in that week, the minister was out hunting: the gun of one of his friends was accidentally discharged in his face, and it blew out both his eyes. He told me that, as he leaned on the butt of that gun, the first thought that came to him was, "All things work together for good to them that love God," and that he did not then, and has not in the twenty years since, felt the least rebellion against God. He has not stopped the practise of his ministry, and all who know him consider his victory over his own misfortune the greatest sermon he has ever preached—and he is preaching it all the time! Perhaps no verse in the whole Bible is better calculated to restore our perspective, in the hour after trouble has come, than this verse. Add your own faith to it, and it transfigures trouble.

One of the commonest kinds of trouble is moods. Some slight thing may have set us off, perhaps nothing has happened at all. But we feel touchy and grouchy. Whatever people say, whatever they do, is wrong. We sit and sulk, we pout at life and circumstances. Maybe we are bilious and need some common medicine: maybe we are really sick and ought to see a doctor. But many times we are simply in the grip of a mood. How shall we break out of it? There is a remarkable story in the life of Jesus, of what He did when a mood of dark despair settled down over Him: it concerned His anticipation of the Cross, which of course was real.[6] But what He did with it can help us all. Study the story carefully. "Now is my soul troubled"—there is the full facing of the fact, with no attempt at cheerful evasion, with no attempt to look on the other side of the Cross to the victory He would make of it: just a plain statement of His anxious heart and mind. "And what shall I say?"—what shall be the way in which I voice this trouble and meet it? There were two courses open: "Father, save me from this hour"—that was the natural, human prayer that asked to be let off the shame and agony of the Cross; but He catches and rights Himself, "But for this cause came I unto this

[6] St. John 12:27ff.

hour"—He remembered His whole purpose in coming into the world, to redeem mankind. "Father, glorify thy name," that was the other and right alternative; He would not ask for what He wanted, He would ask only that the will of God be done. As soon as He had taken this right turning, He felt strength given to Him, as we do. "There came a voice from heaven, saying, I have both glorified it, and will glorify it again." These strengthening messages from God do pour down to those who take His way instead of their own, as all know who have done it: in some way God always fortifies a man in having made a right decision. Now so vivid was this experience that the people standing by said, "It thundered," and others said, "An angel spoke to him." Then, putting Himself wholly outside the role of a human being in need, and speaking not alone as one of us, but as One far beyond us, He said, "This voice came not because of me, but for your sakes. . . ." and He went on to interpret the great event of the Cross which awaited Him. We can follow Him here only in this: that He turned the whole experience to the benefit of others. If we will but let one of our moods pass through the crucible of this incident, we shall not alone leave it well behind us, but it will be found useful to other people later on.

Another kind of trouble that plagues people today is worry. Many people do a thing three times: once when they worry about what to do and how to do it, once when they do it, and once when they worry over having done it the wrong way. Almost everybody with leisure enough to be free from grinding labour finds time to indulge in worry. Frequently it is not too much work that breaks people down, but a normal load of work plus *worry*,—worry is the straw that breaks the camel's back. Indeed, there are people of such conscientiousness that they feel they are not contributing their share to life unless they worry—worry about their families, worry about their finances, worry about the state of the nation and the world. One day when I was trying to help someone who was worrying, I put down: "*Specific for Worry:* (1) Take three minutes in which to face all the facts of your situation; (2) Take another three minutes to accept them as facts, remembering that 'the truth shall make you free'; (3) Remind yourself, in spoken words, that God is able to bring victory to you instead of defeat, and put faith in place of worry; (4) Let Him do this for you now, and then ask Him what He wants you to do next."

The most important thing to say about trouble is that we meet it creatively. We all get up against situations that seem humanly impossible. We have a partner who turns out to be disagreeable or even dishonest. We are married to someone with whom we have less and less in common. The company for which we work is giving short measure to customers and not living up to promises. We'd like to work in the church, but there are some people that don't get along with each other there, and we wonder. Or we know a man or woman who's gone bad, repudiated every responsibility and shocked the town. What shall we do? There are three things we can do with a humanly impossible situation: we can *abjure* it and run away; we can *endure* it and do nothing about it, or we can seek to *cure* it by taking responsibility.

Here is a marriage which began well but has grown loveless and drab. We can abjure it, walk out, get a separation or divorce; we can endure it, pretend everything is all right and go on with a heavy heart and no hope; or we can find an answer to the question why two people who once loved each other love each other no more. A man told me he was getting a divorce. His wife had hurt him, and he had hurt her—irreparably. We talked of these three ways of meeting the situation. If he were to take the third, he would need to find the spiritual answer for his own life first, admit his emotional immaturity, confess to his wife where he had been wrong rather than just accuse her of where she had been wrong. He followed the third course, and they are working it out together.

Here is a business where, in the next office to yours, there sits a man who thinks he does good works, but is really selfish, wants more than his share, crowds you out. You think he is impossible. You can abjure it all, resign, get out, leave him to make another associate as miserable as he has made you. Or you can for safety's sake say nothing and do nothing. Or you can ask God to show you where you may have been wrong, pray for that man, wait for the chance to talk with him, perhaps telling him where you think you might have been more cooperative or unselfish; and ask whether you two cannot find some deeper level of understanding and cooperation. This may lead to a change in him.

Here is someone who has gone off the rails in a big way, scandalized the neighbourhood, maybe gotten in jail for it. There is a type of pharisaical religious person who abjures such individuals, "He is really too terrible for me to have anything to do with him." There is a sentimental religious person who merely endures the situation and says, "I feel sorry for him, but there is nothing I can do." Then there is the real Christian who looks for a cure, who says, "There but for the grace of God go I. I must seek him out in friendship and understand him. I must tell him about the needy places in my own life, and about God's power and forgiveness." Which are we, Pharisees, sentimentalists, or true Christians? Do we abjure and walk away in self-righteous scorn? Do we endure, and take no responsibility at all? Or do we seek to cure, asking God to use us as bridges across which He can walk into the life of that other person in need?

The conclusion of the matter is, then, that trouble comes in some form to all in this mortal life. But some have within them the capacity to transmute trouble into triumph, to see it coming and to know that wrapped within it there is some kind of blessing for somebody. Only a false faith pretends that trouble itself is false: true faith says it is entirely real, but faith knows the victory that overcomes the world. It is fair to say that there can be no happiness unless we can meet trouble with the calmness born of the assurance that the trouble into which God is allowed to come with His creativity and with His consolations is already a transformed trouble. There is nothing in this world more likely to help people find an unbroken happiness than finding that there is a positive way of dealing with trouble.

VII

Satisfying Human Relations

THERE is a story about an old resident of a growing town: he had some philosophy in him, and met, one after the other, two new residents. The first one asked him, "What kind of people live in this town?" To which the old resident replied casually, "Well, what kind of people lived in the town you came from?" "Oh, they were *swell* people," he said, "everybody was friendly and neighbourly: I never saw nicer people in my life." "Well," said the wise old resident, "you'll find we have just the same kind of people here, too." The second newcomer asked the same question, "What kind of people do you have here?" And he was met by the same question, "What kind of people did you have back where you came from?" He said, "They were the most disagreeable people I ever lived amongst in my life: they talked about each other, and there were feuds, and nobody got along." And the old resident had to give the same reply as he gave to the first: "I guess you'll find just the same kind of people here, too."

We tend to find what we look for in other people. This is so true that sometimes it appears that human relations are almost a reflection of our own subjective attitudes, as roadside reflectors light up from our own head-lights. Happy people are nice people to be with, while unhappy ones take it out of you. Happy people are good neighbours, spread good-will and satisfaction, and in turn find themselves at home and satisfied in their communities.

The enjoyment and understanding of people, the cultivation and maintenance of long-range relationships with them, is to some a natural gift; it requires no effort. Indeed sometimes they enjoy people to such a degree that they are miserable if threatened with a couple of hours by themselves. And there are people for whom social companionship is almost like a strong drink, they become positively intoxicated by the presence of a group of attractive and congenial people.

Some of this can be shallow, some of it quite selfish and irresponsible. But we all envy people with these social qualities, for we know they are strong elements in happiness.

But suppose this is not "natural" to us? Suppose we are inclined to live within ourselves, or fail to make contacts which draw people to us easily, or suppose for some reason we even seem to repel people—what then? I suppose the answer is that people who cannot play by ear must learn to play by note. We want in this chapter to put down some of the white and black notes of harmonious human relations.

The first thing I should like to say concerns the almost infinite importance of human relations, not alone for happiness, but for the very progress and safety of the race. War, wherever you cut it, is the same thing—in individuals it is conflict, in homes it is strain and divorce, in business and industry it is strikes and lock-outs, in nations it is sectionalism and group self-interest, between nations it is war. And peace, wherever you find it, is the same thing—in individuals it is adjustment of personality and harmony of qualities, in homes it is understanding and commonly accepted aims, in industry it is mutual respect, consideration and cooperation, in nations it is "justice and freedom for all," between nations it is peace. It may be true that you would not necessarily get peace on earth even if you had great numbers of individuals with peace in their hearts, and great numbers of homes and industries where peace reigned. But one thing is sure:

we shall surely not get peace on earth *unless* we have it in these places. Unless we can manage to make peace a living and on-going thing in the areas small enough, near enough to hand, for us to control them, how can we hope to have peace in the larger world?

Moreover, happy and satisfactory human relations are one of the surest marks of happy, well-adjusted people. Where do psychologists look to find the source of a great deal of the inferiority and neuroticism which plague people today? In their early relations with their families. Far too much is often made of this, as if no one could live down or get beyond these early emotional experiences: but no one can deny their importance. I have watched a good many people who are disturbed, unhappy, ill-adjusted, begin coming out into the daylight of understanding themselves, of increasing happiness, and good adjustment to life; and it is because they begin sending out roots into two soils—the soil of greater faith in God, and the soil of better relations with people. The first step away from despairing self-centeredness is likely to be in the formation of a friendship with one other understanding person. The value of those who are spiritually trained in meeting this widespread need today can hardly be overestimated: there are many with no psychiatric nor theological training, who yet are up-builders of other people, know how to meet them, talk with them, play with them, draw them out of themselves, give them a sense that they matter and can make worthwhile friendships. It is a desolating thing to be without one friend with whom one can talk over the things in life that matter.

We must also remember that people, while at bottom craving much the same thing, differ greatly in temperament, and must be met in each case individually. Some people are like metal, they are cold stuff and they stay cold, no matter what the heat of the common atmosphere may be. Some people are like fur, they quickly respond to the warmth in others, and begin adding to it on contact. Some people are like fire itself, they are warm all the way through, and warm everything they touch with the fire wherewith they themselves are warmed. Let us beware of too superficial and quick judgments about them: have not some whom at first you did not like become later your friends? Instead of letting people rouse in us an instant dislike which makes our hackles stand up, and instead of being too easily swept off our feet by a striking "personality," let us always and with everyone try sending out the antennae of our own understanding, seeking to "get on board" with them, to know what "makes them tick," and talking of what interests them and not only what interests us. Of course we shall venture to mention our interests, for it is by such "feelers" that personalities mesh and become welded together in friendly understanding. But watch the great artists in human relations—they will be more eager to discover what you are thinking about than to tell you what they are thinking about. We need not worry, most of us, about casual human contacts: many of us are flung into the maelstrom of unavoidable human contacts every day. What we do need to be concerned about is two things: (1) how we may form deep and satisfying friendships, that are of mutual enjoyment and benefit, and (2) how people for whom friendship is not a natural art may cultivate it.

A surprising number of people tell me that they are "the kind of people that others pour out their troubles to." They like this—of course they do—it means they have sympathy, at least latent, and it means they are useful and needed. It also means that the world is full of those looking for someone with enough integrity to give one confidence, with enough understanding to listen and hear them out, and with enough experience of life to throw some light on their own questions. Now many, under these highly potential circumstances, say too much, or do not say enough, or say the wrong thing, or go "professional" if they know a little psychology or religion, or create dependents of those who seek them out—there is no end to the mistakes we can make. Neither is there any end to the help we can give if we learn how to ripen acquaintance into friendship and friendship into confidence. We are not out after people like spiders after flies: we simply want to live so happily and cheerfully that these confidences flower out perfectly naturally, and our relationships become rich, creative and fruitful. Not everyone we meet will grow into such a friend: but some will, or should; and we need to be ready for them. They may have much for us, we may have much for them. We seek mutually creative, mutually satisfying relations with them.

If this is to be the case, then we must always regard people as ends, not as means. We often have to look upon ourselves as means, and not be too disturbed if others do, while we are in a creative process of trying to help them: but others must always be ends to us. We must not "use" people, if we would maintain happy, satisfying relations with them. This does not mean that legitimate business may not grow up out of casual contacts, of such a sort as may be mutually useful: but it is to say that if our human relations are to be what they should, there must come into them something very close to reverence for other personalities. The more we accept our friends and acquaintances, not as accidental pick-ups, but as providentially given to us for some good purpose—and the more we make of our relationships, not two dots at the end of a line, but rather two angles at the base of a triangle, with God the great Friend at the apex, the more we shall bring into our relationships the freedom and spaciousness which is farthest from utility and domination, and the creativity which will make them not only happy but productive of their highest usefulness. The more our relationships are permeated with the Christian spirit of caring and of expectation and of service, the happier they will be.

For many of us, the problem is what to do with an unsatisfactory, a strained or even a broken, relationship. A minor irritation arises from some habit which a member of the family does not think it worth-while to break. We have never quite been able to "meet" a relative or acquaintance, whom we do not understand and who we feel does not understand us. Perhaps a real wrong has been done somewhere, the other person has gotten more than his share of an inheritance, or there has been a sharp trade, or an unkind truth or unkind untruth has been told and spread about us. Or an old bone of contention lies between two people: they never quite pick it up and deal with it, but every time one of them starts for it, there is a flare-up and the likelihood of a "scene." Can anything be done to repair such a relationship? Yes, I think it can.

The first thing is to remember our own faults. Maybe we think this situation entirely caused by the fault of the other person: and perhaps it has been. What about the spirit with which we have met it—has that been faultless? Do the irritations make us irritable? Have we met the real wrong of another by another kind of wrong of our own,—anger, harsh words, self-righteousness, perhaps some words said just where they will do the most harm? Wordly-wise de la Rochefoucauld reminds us that "Quarrels would not last long if the fault was only on one side."[1] We ought always to receive the wrongs that others do, mindful

[1] *Maxim,* p. 496.

that we have done similar things and will probably do them again—and that there is likely someone else who has good cause to feel about us the way we are feeling toward the person we think has wronged us. I go so far as to say that, in the Providence of God, it is quite likely we are in some sense guilty of provoking this particular wrong in this particular person, and that we may need precisely this test to reveal a weakness in ourselves that needs attention. If we are constantly thinking of our rights and others' wrongs, we shall get nowhere: if we remember their rights and our wrongs, we shall make progress.

Second, if this condition is not to go on, flaring up sometimes, subsiding at others, we must one day go to the mat and have it all out in the open. It does no good to peck at it by nagging, by oblique reference, by sarcasm, by the tears of "injured innocence." There is a real "right" in the situation somewhere, God's absolute right. If we are mindful of our own faults, deeply so; and if we speak with humility in our hearts, one of us may, in spite of all our faults, more nearly approximate the point of view of God than the other does for the moment, just as a nation which may be far from perfect may have to take up arms against another whose evil is potentially more devastating for humankind. If this be yourself, try to keep your temper as far as possible, and speak justly and fairly only of those things which are demonstrable as facts: then have your say. Pray about it before hand, seek to make the occasion, not one when you win the day, but one when the Spirit of God comes anew into both of you; but, with this preparation, let what you feel come out. It will be painful, alike to the other person and to yourself. There may be protestations of innocence, and efforts at self-justification: hold by your point and prove your case by facts, not general accusations. If need be, bring in a third person who may be involved, and get him to stand up to the truth with you. Give in where you know you are wrong: you are seeking the truth, and you are seeking to mend a severely strained relation—so keep from irrelevant things, from exaggeration, from trying to gain a point at every stage in the conversation. Try to maintain the relationship itself throughout, remembering the pain and shame and confusion and anger in the other person, all which things will be there till the truth you are trying to stand for has its effect. It must come through a person—yourself—that is understanding, conscious of his own faults, deeply redemptive. But it is "the truth that makes you free"; you must deal in the truth. And throughout, remember that you are not to be a critic, a carper, a Pharisee lording it over someone else: but you must be mature in what Dr. Fritz Kunkel calls "the great test of maturity: if necessary, to inflict consciously and conscientiously pain and sacrifice upon our most beloved friends."[2] If our own spirits are right, the net effect of all this is positive, redemptive, healing.

[2] *In Search of Maturity,* p. 285.

Third, this will cause the other person to shift position, if it has been well and rightly done; and that involves a great blow to his pride, of which we must be conscious. Let us not seek to soften the blow itself, for it may be needed by him, as it often is needed by us. For such an operation, we need the anaesthetic of love and great understanding. We are not so much seeking to make him "do" something we want, nor take our advice—John Keith Benton says truly that "Giving advice is an expression of pride, not of good-will."[3] We are seeking to help the person recognize and dislodge a viewpoint, a way of dealing or speaking, a false value. Again and again we must confess our own inadequacy, shortcomings, sins, to keep the record honest. We are not his critic or his judge: we are only his helper, who speaks, not from authority nor "right," but simply as a fellow-sinner. If we are to carry this process through with mature discrimination and redemptive intent and effect, we must ourselves have absorbed the wisdom of Walt Whitman's questions, "Have you learned lessons only of those who admired you, and were tender with you, and stood aside for you? Have you not learned great lessons from those who rejected you, and braced themselves against you, or disputed the passage with you?"[4] This will keep us humble, while we stand courageously by the truth,

[3] *Clinical Pastoral Training,* p. 86.

[4] Quoted in *Democracy in Action,* by S. Morrison and E. P. Wilson.

and seek winningly as well as firmly to get lodgment for it in the minds of others.

Fourth, the person you seek to help may acknowledge that you are right. It may come in a sob of penitent sorrow and a request for forgiveness. It may come in a general admission, "Maybe there is something in what you say: I never knew it before." Maybe you will not have the satisfaction of any admission of agreement with you: but it will come out in a changed attitude and way of acting and living. The "soreness" may be there for a while, as it is after a physical operation; but begin at once rebuilding the relationship closer than ever, with friendship, thoughtfulness, appreciation, and where possible cooperation. If it is possible to heal it all up in prayer together, that is the best place and way to do it. Prayer seems to remove the last traces of personal sting, and to send the relationship renewed and made over out upon new ways of discovery.

Sometimes, if one is to help, he must try to mediate between two people who are estranged. This is delicate business, especially if one's advice has not been asked: then one must "feel his way" with great tact and caution. But there are laws that apply here, too.

One of them is: don't take sides, take responsibility. And that means taking sides with the truth, but not with persons. It means we shall side with the right in each person (and there will probably be some of it), it means we shall side against the wrong in each person (and there will be some of that, too). We shall not give all our sympathy to the person with whom we talk at the moment, but remember there is another person to hear: we shall keep our counsel and suspend our judgment. We shall notice those qualities in the person with whom we are talking that could lead to trouble and misunderstanding, being mindful of the person whose "side" we have not yet heard. It is our first aim to learn the facts—the facts of the situation, and the facts about the people involved in it. We must not add a third lot of emotions, but keep ourselves detached while we are concerned and interested. Sometimes you cannot unravel all the facts talking to the two involved people separately, and it is better to get them together. One who is fair and just, who has insight and a capacity for objective consideration, can be a kind of umpire or arbiter who may for the first time provide two differing people with a practical way of approach to one another. How many times have I sat with a husband and wife who thought they were in inextricable difficulties, patiently heard first one side, then the other; then got them together and asked them to say in the presence of the other person all they had said behind his or her back. The "airing" is often much needed: the frank explanation of what it is that irritates or outrages us. But how often, too, has undiluted judgment of the other person become tempered by this time with the awareness (often the new awareness) of one's own faults. This is a surprise and sometimes a delight to the other person, who never expected to hear the husband or wife admit anything, but only looked for criticism and self-justification! One wants to do a little sharing of his own experience in such a situation, and not to give the impression that he is above mistakes and faults in human relations himself. There wants to be some humour with all this, for that saving salt may have been absent for a long time. When each person sees that he or she is at least in part responsible for the situation, when a kind of cool reasonableness has come into the atmosphere in place of the heat of anger and hopelessness, it may be a good time for you to leave the room for a while, and let them have a good cry together and get melted back into the beginnings of a new unity. It may look at times during the conversation as if you had let loose factors that threaten any reconciliation whatever; but hold by your moral and spiritual ideals, remember that these are working all the time on both parties, keep praying and quietly confident throughout, and the results may surprise you!

I have dealt at some length with what might be called a "technique of reconciliation," because I believe that nothing is more terribly needed. It would be idle to go on uttering platitudes about human relationships in a book on happiness, if one did not face the fact that many human relations are decidedly unhappy and that unless they can be repaired and restored there is no happiness for the contracting parties. Part of the soul-sickness of our time lies in severed and seemingly irreparable relationships: it multiplies in the lives that are touched by these separated and guilty people, especially their children. There would come a whole new hope about humanity and the world at large if some of the relationships, now headed for the rocks, could be steered round them and safely started for the open sea of understanding and happiness. We do not have much hope for humanity so long as we feel incorrigible ourselves: we do not have great expectations of the United Nations Organization if we cannot get two young people to put mature and responsible unselfishness in place of the often immature and irresponsible selfishness of divorce. And what one says of domestic difficulties and reconciliations applies equally to all other areas of life. The world's peace and unity needs the foundation of reconciled relations all through the body of humanity, as a smooth highway rests upon millions of little stones that have been moulded into solidity and harmony.

And now, to come back to the more ordinary problems of daily human relations, let us apply to them some of the insights which we know about human nature and society.

It is important, I think, to find our own levels in friendship, and to learn how to be creative instead of dissatisfied with them. Many a girl has suffered acutely from the fact that her mother wished to make her a "social success," when actually she is a serious, intellectual, scientific or some other type of person. There may be only unhappiness if we live under pressure from ourselves or from others to "get in" where we do not, in any deep sense, belong: we all find greater satisfaction, ordinarily, from our own kind. But we may need to come to a much more imaginative and creative view of the people of our own level. For instance, I remember meeting a serious lad from a Northern university, with a pretty bad inferiority complex: he had not made a fraternity, and was not likely to be socially popular anywhere. I asked him whether there were other fellows at college in somewhat his situation, and he thought for a moment and said he thought there were. I put up to him going back to be a real missionary to the lonely men on the campus: the idea invigorated him, gave him hope, put light in his eyes! He went back and did it, and found life a different thing for him. We need a purpose running through our social relations, if they are really to be satisfying.

There is much in the old adage about "give and take." Some people want to be dominators, and some want to be door mats: the former get satisfaction in bossing, the latter in being bossed. We must lift these parodies of "give and take" to the real thing. We meet few people to whom we may not give something, if it be only a good story: with some we should give much more—an interest, a sincere compliment, a generalization that may happen to hit the spot for them, a word with an edge to it spoken with a wink of understanding, some information they need or some contact we can make for them. But it is bad for us to be always on the "giving" end: we need to be also on the "receiving" end as well. Many do not perceive the lurking pride that often lies behind the ostensible unselfishness of always wanting to pay the check and never be under obligations to anyone else. Some people need to say a genuine "Thank you" more than they need to say the General Confession! We ought always to be watching for the wisdom we need, the corrective, the enlargement of view-point, that may come through another person. How little do we see or understand ourselves! And how true it is, as Dr. Jung says, ". . . we must admit that everyone else probably understands us better than we understand ourselves."[5] We do not need to creep about as if we had no right to live, or obsequiously were seeking the assistance of others: but we ought to be constantly mindful of the mutual enrichment that is intended when two people become friends. Let us look for the chances to "give and take."

Surely many in our time have got exactly twisted their emphasis upon tolerance and intolerance. How very often we are lax toward those moral ideals which are so essential, not only to our own, but to all human happiness, and "tolerant" when we or others treat them casually! And how often are we ready to stiffen up into great intolerance toward people we do not like,

[5] *Modern Man in Search of a Soul,* p. 88.

especially groups of people to whom we assign certain qualities that are offensive to us! What we *need* is a great intolerance toward the moral laxity that is the most threatening sign in our day, especially as we see it emerging in ourselves: and a great tolerance toward all human beings, mindful that insofar as they are identified with any actual wrongdoing we must withstand them as well as it, but that they must be won away from their wrongdoing, not only by the just pressure of public opinion, but by the gentle suasion of private friendliness and help. The things we rightly dislike in individuals and groups as they dislike them in us is *sin*—sin which sometimes takes characteristic forms in certain types of personality and even certain racial groups. Do you not, when you hear Gentiles condemning Jews, for instance, or when you hear Jews looking to be white-washed as if they never did anything wrong at all, say to yourself Bobbie Burns' famous lines,

> "Wad some power the giftie gie us
> To see oursel'es as ithers see us"?

It is a difficult balance to maintain, putting our tolerance and our intolerance in the right place. There is a time to stand up so completely and courageously for what is right that we would threaten any human relation by it: and there is a time to keep so closely identified with a human being who may be doing wrong, that the world thinks we are condoning what he is doing even when we are not! Let us seek and pray for this balance to be ours.

We must learn to achieve a balance, too, in where we accept and where we resist people. There is a philosophy of life and of human happiness which will sacrifice anything to the ease and comfort and immediate peace of the relationship: this is utterly and completely immoral. Few human relations are worth anything that are uniformly and unbrokenly happy. Their true happiness consists in their willingness and ability to go through occasional periods of unhappiness, fruitfully and creatively met, in order to grow and to come out with the larger kind of happiness in the end. A relationship that is all sugar, and never has any salt in it, is an immoral relationship. Human beings not only "get away with murder" when they can count on such dealings from others, but they may live in ignorance of the truth that saves. The salt of truth and resistance now and then keeps respect within a relationship; and if it is done without pride and without self-satisfaction, it will not lessen the affection of the relationship, either.

Yet with all this, we need a large measure of forgivingness in all our relations. Those with a strong sense of justice often find it too hard to forgive, while those who care very much about the relationships as such may find it too easy. The longer I watch people, the more do I conclude that many of them have never learned how to live. When I see children brought up in ignorance of that spiritual truth and moral righteousness from which alone came their parents' integrity, not to say the foundation of our civilization itself, I wonder what folly animates the fathers and mothers: for in the end, this means such selfishness in the child as will fail somewhere in life's chief responsibilities, and stand in need of that very spiritual strength which has been lacking. One deplores this: yet one needs to be very understanding of the individual who, after this process has had its way, finds himself or herself bewildered, without moorings, and needing a guiding hand. For the many mistakes people make toward us, remembering how many we make toward them, we need a large charity, not too sharp a memory, and a good "forgetery." A wonderful old Southern servant, writing as best she could to an absent mistress, apologized for her errors of grammar and penmanship, adding, "Jes take all the mistakes for love." We can afford to do this far more often than we do.

Perhaps there never was given a better recipe for happy human relations than is included in the description of the Quakers which George Fox gave, when writing from Domesdale jail, where he was imprisoned for his faith:

"Friends walk cheerfully over the earth, answering that of God in every man."

VIII

The Overflow of Happiness

IT TAKES only the slightest observation of people to realize that, as unhappiness slows them down, dries up the wells of resource, turns off the supply of creative ideas and energy, happiness does just the opposite, it tones up the whole personality and not only uses to the full but distends and increases all its capacities. We have all been wishing, I suppose, that some great positive, beneficent influence might sweep the nations and the world for good, as the dictatorships and totalitarianism swept them for evil. We remember that Hitler got going in an unhappy nation, and produced his frightful effects by speaking to and working upon and organizing the unhappiness of his people. We see at once the possible connection between the good adjustment and happiness of large numbers of people, and the peace and safety of the world.

Let us now consider some of the effects of happiness in the human heart, its overflow in personalities and in society.

The first is apt to be release and freedom that has profound manifestations in the whole physical and psychological system. When one has perceived and applied a spiritual truth, this effect is sometimes tremendous. George Fox, after a profound spiritual experience, wrote in his journal, "All things were new; and all the creation gave another smell unto me than before, beyond what words can utter."[1] The use of the word "smell" is significant: does not one catch the wonder of mountain air largely through drawing in the breath and imbibing deeply of the ozone in it—and is not this a perfect parallel of what happens when the spirit gets up into the upper ether of the heights? Not long ago a young officer came back from five years of over-seas duty. He looked well, yet there was an indefinable strain about him. Sometimes he would shake with "jitters" and his nerves were in poor shape. He had some medical tests made, and the doctor told him these did not match up with his nervous condition: physically he was in good shape. First the doctor recommended a year's rest in the South: later he said to the officer, "I believe you are afraid of these shakes of yours, and the fear is what brings them on. Go ahead and shake if you want to." An hour later the officer was on a plane, and it came over him strongly that this was the case: it was his fear that was keeping him back and causing him to suffer these attacks of nerves. So he thereupon turned the fear over to God absolutely. There stole over him a wonderful peace, such as he had not felt in years, perhaps such as he had never felt; for in such an experience we often let go

[1] George Fox. *Journal,* p. 25.

of *ourselves* to God more deeply than ever before. This was not a momentary emotion: I saw him some hours later and remarked that his face looked less strained than I had seen it since he got back. A letter from him says, "There is something too wonderful about feeling the old soul free again without a dark shadow over it—that is what I have been feeling ever since that experience on the plane. It's still here, and with the help of God, it will stay. It made an instantaneous difference in my relations at home. I went to sleep last night and had the best sleep I have had since I got back. I have just had to sing for half an hour. It's *wonderful*, and the old nerves have quieted right down. I could go on singing for the happiness that is in me: I feel as though I had come up out of a black dark hole into the sun again." When the fear which was the block to release and happiness was given over to God in an act of decision, the release and happiness came about. An event like that is not only personal and private: it is positively scientific in that it instances universal law. Millions might have experiences like that, if they grasped what that man has grasped!

Happiness has immeasurable effects upon health. It must be freely admitted that good glands can be a source of temperamental happiness: but it must be realized, too, that happiness is very good for the glands and the rest of the body! As shock, fear, disappointment cut down bodily well-being, so faith, confidence and happiness increase it. There are times when spiritual faith produces cures that appear to be nothing less than miracles; there are times when it produces the calmness and quietness of spirit in which steady healing can better take place; and there are times when it produces the courage and serenity which takes bodily limitation or pain in the right spirit and will not be downed by them. Health is often manifested in energy and capacity for work: these are greatly increased by the happiness that comes from faith. A doctor, now close to eighty, is a radiant example of this kind of health and strength born of joy and faith. For fifty years he has not had a vacation (except for one illness), he makes from forty to fifty personal calls or telephone calls a day, his interest in his people seems as much pastoral as medical, he seldom speaks of himself or refers to himself, but lives with a great faith burning in his heart which comes out in an overflowing love for people. Perhaps he began with a good frame, I do not know: but surely he has gotten the best work out of his body because of obedience to the laws of God and through the faith that fills him with happiness and pours out into the lives that he touches.

There is also, I believe, a connection between happiness and integrity of the deeper kind. Not all happy people are good, and not all good people are happy, because they may be looking for happiness in the wrong place. But the genuinely happy person is a well-integrated person, using the word in its psychological sense: and there is a connection between this and "integrity" used in the moral sense. Clearly, it is better to be good, even if you have to fight yourself to do it, than not to be good at all: but clearly, also, it is better to be good because you want to, because you have found a new motive for doing so, and because the right kind of attitudes and conduct pour out of you in a joyous understanding that they are themselves an integral part of happiness. There is a kind of conscientious, "good" person, who seems not to have found the real source either of goodness or of happiness: and there is a kind of person who has come to terms with God, with life, with themselves, and who enter enthusiastically into the adventure of existence, for whom integrity is the natural expression of an adjusted and integrated nature. A deeply "moral" act is not alone one which if repeated by everyone would result in good, it is not only one which considers the welfare of others, or even seeks to fulfil the laws of God: a deeply "moral" act is one in which, beside these things, the whole personality is deeply convinced and completely given. In this sense, only an integrated person *can* really be good. Time was when many people were "good" because they thought they ought to be, or feared hell-fire if they weren't, but their whole souls seemed not to be in it: latterly we have seen a great moral slump, many doing exactly as they please, refusing (as they often say) to be "hypocritical" about their actions. They have something, these folk who believe that what we do should express what we really feel and are: but often their need is to realize that there is a great deal more to life than what they like to do; and if it is to go on becoming more and more of a satisfying adventure, they will have to come to terms with all of it, including the moral tradition of the race, and the need to consider the full effect of one's acts. It is this inner integration that spells so large a part of happiness, and which issues in integrity of life.

The outside of happiness is generally cheerfulness. The professional cheer-monger is a pest, and the frozen smile one of the great shams of our time. But people who like to laugh, who see the funny side of things, who turn up the corners of their mouths at slight provocation, and do the day's work with occasional spurts of playfulness, are public benefits. One reason why I happen to like Boston terriers is that they are always ready to play—a quick motion, a playful note in your voice, will set them off at any time. Well, I like people with that same spring-like quality in them, and I think most of us do. We admire those who seek to be cheerful when we know they are not happy—when they are going through an illness, or have experienced a great disappointment or loss; but this is a temporary matter. At ordinary times, we sense it very definitely when people try to be cheerful on the outside when they are not happy within—they smile with their lips but not with their eyes, they tell jokes but they are not mirthful, something sharp and bitter so often spoils their intended humour. Somehow you cannot "fake" cheerfulness: it only has its largest effect on others when it is the outward side of genuine happiness. When one thinks of the amount of cheer that people seek to purchase outside of themselves—in bottles, in theater tickets, in expensive journeys, and remember how much of this is not the expression of happiness but precisely flight from its dreaded opposite, one values the true cheerfulness that comes up out of the merry heart. Nothing is more delightful to live with, and nothing is more contagious. I am convinced that some children grow up solemn and humourless because their homelife is like that, while others learn to love humour, laughter and fun, because they have it round them when they are young. Neither in a home nor in a life can there be cheerfulness except when things are "right": when there are faith, open and loving relationships, and purpose, cheerfulness is natural and perhaps inevitable.

One of the things that people need most is to find satisfaction in life's commonplace things, in what we often call "the daily grind." It has been found, for instance, that a large number of house-wives dislike their house-work. One wonders how much of this comes from that rather disastrous view of work—manual, menial work—which seems to have been sedulously cultivated in this country during recent years? One wonders how much of it comes from a feeling that a woman working in the house—cleaning, cooking, washing—is a kind of beast of burden, while the veriest little flapper punching type-writer keys or operating a switch-board is a step nearer being a "professional woman"? There is, I am afraid, a wide-spread desire to get something for nothing, to be well-paid for a minimum of work, to live on the labour of other people: it is a false philosophy, it is the opposite of the philosophy that built up America, it is akin to alien philosophies which would undermine our liberties if they could. So we need to change our thinking about the place of work in general—then we may get a better view of our work in particular. But nothing greases the wheels of labour like contentment in the heart, nothing can make a day's work fly faster than to feel that in the doing of it we are serving those whom we love, accomplishing something that needs doing in the world, and above all that through the spirit in which we work something of the creative Spirit of God is released into the world. For instance, if a housewife is conscious that the tone she sets in the home can make or break the work-day of her husband, that she more than anyone else creates the cheerfulness and encouragement which makes her children successful at school, both as to books and as to friends, her "housework" takes on a new significance, and she may begin to find a new tingle and thrill in "the trivial round, the common task." If a man in a factory has always at the back of his mind his love for a family whom he is supporting, if he feels that his part of even a drudging task is caught up into significance when it is brought together with what others do, so that the whole product is something to be proud of and grateful for, because of what it means in the life of the community and the nation and the world, then the "daily grind" is transformed. When a person is happy, the emotion of happiness itself seems to empty out of the glands fresh streams of energy, just as it fills the mind with a new sense of worthwhile-ness. You can almost feel these discharges of physical energy into your system. In the setting of a God-intended, God-planned life, with all eternity before you, one sees the place of washing dishes, mending socks, driving trucks and laying bricks. If one is to meet a tiring, daily duty, or carry through a common-place job, one needs a big view of life itself, and one needs the fresh springs of contentment and energy that bubble up out of a happy life. However much or little imagination the task itself may require, the relationships with people which arise through the job take all the imagination we can muster. It is usually in these that people find the opportunities for service and usefulness and enjoyment that make the day's work go swiftly, and make some of us wish it had forty-eight hours in it instead of twenty-four!

The kind of real happiness of which we are speaking issues also in a clearer sense of one's duty. Much of the confusion and unhappiness of our time consists in bewilderment about what we ought to do, what is right, what constitutes our duty. Unhappy people are often so taken up with their own states of mind, with fighting against moods, other people or circumstances that seem set against them, that instead of making clear-cut decisions they are often pushed by the conditions or even the pressure of time to do the next thing as best they can—with the result that there is no over-all plan to their lives, they become the very pawn of circumstances which they most hate to be! It is easy enough, if we are honest, to tell right from wrong: it is not always easy to know which of several perfectly proper courses we ought to take, or to weigh all the considerations that should affect a decision. But those who are happy with the happiness that comes from being in league with God, know that God has a plan for them, a big, over-all plan for His world, but also a personal plan for them. They know that He will help them to see, if not the whole pattern, at least the next necessary step. A verse like "Commit thy way unto the Lord; trust also in him; and he shall bring it to pass"[2] becomes their stay and stand-by. Such people feel the same first-thought of concern as we all feel, facing a new situation that may call for an adequate decision. But they are free of the fear that holds many all the time, and of the ambition to please everybody by what they do. They are free from those accumulated conflicts which obscure the vision for so many, and are free within to follow what seems right with

2 Psalm 37:5.

their whole minds. When we know that the ultimate responsibility lies with God, and that all we have to do is to take the way which the Inner Voice indicates to us, a great weight falls from us, and there comes an increasing sense of what we should do. "If any man will do his will, he shall know . . ."[3] there is the great recipe for finding what we should do: the emphasis is upon "willing" as a prerequisite to the intellectual clarity needed for a right decision. We are happy when we are at leisure from ourselves: and only then do we see what course we ought to take.

Another overflow of happiness is a new way of taking our own sufferings in this world, and of helping others to take theirs. We have already seen that happiness is almost independent of suffering, and may exist right in the middle of it. Those whose happiness is founded on a rock will experience the same blows and sufferings as come to others, for faith does not provide exemption from suffering but only from defeat at its hands; but underneath will still run the current of a deeper happiness which nothing can shake nor take away. There is a "joy that seeketh us through pain": do you remember this fine passage in Amiel's *Journal*,[4] "To lose one's life that one may gain it, to possess nothing that one may conquer all, to renounce self that God may give Himself to us, how impossible a problem, and how sublime a reality! No one truly

[3] St. John 7:17.
[4] P. 55, Mrs. Humphry Ward's translation.

knows happiness who has not suffered, and the redeemed are happier than the elect."

This new view of human suffering does not only give us fresh personal courage: it extends also to the great tragedies of the world at large, of which we have seen and are seeing so many in our time. A greatly courageous Dutch woman, who was in a German concentration camp, now writes, "In a concentration camp, where you see around you living skeletons, the slaying and tormenting of fellow-people, the misery of thousands, and you know that this is only one of the concentration camps of Germany and that there are, moreover, the bombarded cities, the battlefields, the oppressed nations also, then the distress of the world becomes such a terrible reality that you can hardly bear it. Once I knew such a moment. Then I opened my little Bible which I had smuggled in with me. . . . I turned to a page in the book of Isaiah, and read, 'He has borne our sorrows.' Then I understood that we do not need to bear the sorrows of the world. We can't do it, either; only One can do it, Jesus Christ; and He said, when He bore that sorrow on the Cross, 'It is finished.' Then I learned still more. I saw that we are not even allowed to bear the sorrows of the world, for if we do that we do not keep enough of the joy of life to help where we are called."[5] This woman did heroic work for those about her, keeping up their spirits, keeping the very life in them by faith and hope, serving

[5] *The Calvary Evangel,* July 1946, p. 310, b. St. Matthew 6:33.

in every way she could—do not think that this faith of hers produced in her *indifference* to the sorrows of the world about her. It was because she did not grieve and groan uselessly about the tragedy she and those about her were suffering, but left the "burden" of all this to her Lord, that her emotions were free to be employed in serving them. Great belief, leading to great happiness within, finds a place for tragedy, knows how to meet it, knows how to let joy come even into the midst of it. Can anything else do this?

Happiness of the kind we are describing creates in one who has it a great desire that all others, all over the world, should share in it. The truly happy long to spread the happiness they know. When people sit down to enjoy their spiritual happiness, they are on the way to losing it: when they rise up to spread it as far and wide as they can, it increases. This was the desire that lay in the heart of Jesus Christ: He wanted to build in the world something which He called "the kingdom of God" or "the kingdom of heaven." The fulfilment of that vision absorbed all His life and sent Him willingly to His Cross: it was the passion that burned ever in His heart, the objective for which He, and all who caught this passion from Him, were willing to sacrifice everything. That kingdom envisioned the supply of all man's needs through putting the will of God before all else in his life. "Seek ye first the Kingdom of God, and His righteousness," He said, "and all these things shall be added unto you." The perfection of life for which He looked will not be universal, or even wide-spread, in any foreseeable time; but those who are swept with the passion that swept Him are not so much concerned with what *cannot* be done, as with what *can* be done—to that they give themselves without ceasing. It is the task of the Christian Church to implement Jesus' vision for the Kingdom. Each of us has his part in that Kingdom when he or she finds the plan of God for life, and begins to fulfil it. Sometimes we fear how far it would take us, if we gave in to God entirely, and asked Him what He wanted us to do. There are some hard jobs in the world, and He wants somebody to volunteer to go and do them. Hardly anyone has ever done the will of God without somewhere making a costly renunciation, some real surrender of self-will, in order that God's will should prevail. Yet how different does it all look *after* one has made such a decision! A letter lies on my desk from a young woman who is going out to China as a medical research assistant, which says: "One of the serious problems that presented itself to me, as a part of making a real decision for Christ, was a fear that kept going round in my head somewhat like this: 'The trouble with telling God you will obey Him *absolutely* is that He might in an odd moment tell you you had to go off and be a missionary in *China*, than which nothing could be more awful.' But here I am going off to do that thing, which now seems so wonderful but then seemed so dreadful! God has such winsome ways with us!" That person is overflowing with happiness, with the radiance that comes from faith. Her life is going to count in the extension of the Kingdom to one vast potential country, which needs the assistance of medicine, and also of Christian faith. Some who read these words, perhaps, need to make a decision very much like hers. It may seem a great hurdle at first, as it did to her: but in the end it will become a great adventure, as more and more we realize that happiness is not something we grasp and hug and keep, but something we receive and give and share!

The vision, the espousal, and the service of the Kingdom are really the greatest of all the beneficent overflows of happiness, if we have found the kind of happiness that can belong to all men everywhere, and cannot be taken from them by any circumstance that can arise. Such people come up against evil, disappointment, frustration, in forms far more concrete than any others, yet they continue to be the happiest people on earth.

There are two very important footnotes to the great Kingdom, which have especial relevance for our time. One of them is freedom, and the other is world-peace. I believe, and should like to point out, that personal happiness of the kind we are describing here has its part in both.

It has been proven beyond dispute, I should say, that the liberal, democratic process is the only method by which it is possible to preserve the gains of the past and yet make progress toward the future. There is nothing more romantic and fascinating than the zig-zag process by which one course is tried, its goodness discovered, its weakness and out-worn-ness later discovered, and it is discarded for another course which thereupon is treated in the same way. This calls for a very high order of atmosphere, if it is to be made to work at all—a spirit of good sport and fair play, a patience and faith that men can better work out their own salvation than any others can do it for them. But whence comes this high view of man as not alone deserving liberty, but as capable of not misusing it? In our country, at least, it came from two sources: the eighteenth century "enlightenment" philosophy, with its roots in the Greek view of life; and the Christian spirit of our founding fathers. I believe that the individualism of our liberty is largely due to the "enlightenment," and that the responsibility of it is largely due to our Christian heritage. We know that man cannot separate himself from his physical and biological inheritance: how then should he expect to separate himself from his spiritual inheritance? If democracy is, as William Allen White once said it is, "a rough attempt to institutionalize the Christian religion," then must not these two things—the Christian religion, and democratic government—walk always side by side and hand in hand? We must not think there was never Christian government till democracy came along, or that there can never be again: nor must we believe that

Christianity is in any deep sense dependent on democracy. It is just the other way round: democracy is dependent on Christianity! The impulse to liberty is human—all men have it somewhere in their consciousness: but the impulse to use liberty responsibly, so that it may not lead to license, and hence call forth some power that will in the end destroy it—this is a high achievement which belongs to the Christian tradition. All who ride the railroads, read the newspapers, drive the cars, vote in the elections, of this nation are living upon the fruits of past faith in God. There is nothing of "perpetual motion" in democracy: it can arise and then die because it is misused and misunderstood. Are we not in the greatest danger of this today? Are there not thousands, yes, millions of our people who are seeing how far they can go, how much they can get, out of this nation for themselves, ignoring the replenishing of those wells of faith and conviction out of which America's greatness came? Beyond any question, we are the happiest nation on earth. We have many problems unsolved, many people in great need, much that is wrong; but for all that, we are the happiest nation on earth. We are also the richest. Is there not grave question whether we can maintain this position of ours unless other nations are helped to find our kind of wealth, our kind of happiness? We have helped stave off famine in most places of the world: but the next step is to help the peoples of the world to build up their own economy, to find markets for outlets, to develop their own resources. If we would share with them our scientific "know-how," and enable them to develop the processes of liberty within their own borders and in their own way, Communism would not have a look-in anywhere on the face of the earth! But if we are selfish, enjoy our happiness to ourselves, are indifferent to the development of other less privileged nations, can we long hope to enjoy the safety, the wealth, the happiness which we enjoy now? Let us share some of this happiness, or we shall surely lose it! Many are so tied up in themselves, preoccupied with their own worries, busy with their own problems, that they will not give attention to these things. Only the believing and the happy will feel this obligation, and want to be in position to fulfil it.

And then world-peace. Do we understand what peace is? Peace is always a dynamic thing, not a static one. It is not represented by a "contented cow," but by a smooth-flowing river, a perfectly ordered machine, or a good, working team of people. It is represented by ordered motion, not by the stillness of stagnancy. Now in motion there is always friction. Peace does not mean the absence of all friction; for that would be the absence of all life and all progress. Without disagreement there would never be progress, the best would never challenge the accepted, the ideal never supplant the actual. Real peace in a democratic country does not mean universal agreement and unity: this would be as undesirable as it would be impossible.

It means gladly keeping the ways open for frank criticism, for news and information to be spread abroad, for all to have their say without fear or favour, so that in the end the best light of the majority may hold sway till better light begins to shine and is given its chance to lighten the whole. There is a kind of family peace and unity which, held too long, becomes monopoly and then dictatorship. If there are no disagreements in the family, it usually means that somebody has got the upper hand and is keeping it because everybody else is afraid to dissent! Peace means the spirit in which all can be free to seek the highest and best together, and the will to follow it when it is seen. Peace, in the home, in the nation, and in the world, means "disagreement without being disagreeable." We must insist that the ways be kept open for change, dissent, progress, in our post-war arrangements, else we shall most surely "lose the peace."

And we come back to the same truth about peace, as we found about happiness. Peace is a by-product. When you pursue it for itself, it eludes you. Nations concentrated on making and keeping peace are likely to war as to methods and procedures. But when you are doing what you ought, when you ought, in the way you ought, when your life or the life of your nation is geared to the will of God, when your human relations are dominated by the aims of love and service, you suddenly wake up to the fact that life is going extraordinarily well, and you are being exceptionally happy and peaceful. When you pursue peace or happiness, you are centered in yourself: all you get is an occasional respite from misery. But when you do what you should, by God and other people, you seem to get happiness and peace thrown in as a wonderful gratuity. The peace of the world, like that of the individual, is a by-product. When nations ostensibly seek the peace of the world, but are at the same time pursuing their own selfish ways, their own form of power in the world (and all nations tend to do this), then talk of peace is a mockery. But when nations do what they ought, when they ought, in the way they ought, when the will of God is allowed to emerge in national life, causes of friction tend to disappear.

This is not all abstract theory. After the Boxer Uprising in China, America exacted twenty million dollars of indemnity. One of the great missionaries of another generation, Dr. Arthur H. Smith, went to President Theodore Roosevelt and suggested that the money, when paid, be returned to China for an indemnity college and for scholarships to train young Chinese in this country. This was done. How much of friendship has that little twenty million brought to us, because we recognized China's need, and entered into it with one really Christian gesture! A similar case has been our treatment of the Philippines: from the beginning our aim has been their help in every phase of their life, and finally their freedom. Nations can do, and have done, the Christian thing. They have not done it often enough to secure peace in the world.

All through the Bible peace is looked upon as the fruit of righteousness. So many people want the fruit without the root! If we sought the Kingdom and the righteousness first, the peace might be ours as a by-product. I do not see how anyone can have much hope for the peace of the world until men realize that peace is not just a lull in which they may pursue still more feverishly their own selfish aims and plans, but peace is both that product and that potentiality which is given to men and nations that do the will of God. Peace is happiness within and between nations. Statesmen alone cannot create it: it comes to nations through people who know that happiness does not mean getting everything you want, but doing what God wants you to do with your circumstances. And so, whether we speak of personal happiness, or of world-peace we accept as the conclusion of the whole matter the great word of Dante:

"In His will is our peace."